Iterating Infusion

Clearer Views of Objects, Classes, and Systems

GREG ANTHONY

apress®

Iterating Infusion: Clearer Views of Objects, Classes, and Systems

Copyright © 2012 by Greg Anthony

ISBN 978-1-4302-5104-0

ISBN 978-1-4302-5105-7 (eBook)

President and Publisher: Paul Manning
Lead Editor and Technical Reviewer: Jonathan Hassell
Editorial Board: Steve Anglin, Mark Beckner, Ewan Buckingham, Gary Cornell, Louise Corrigan, Morgan Ertel, Jonathan Gennick, Jonathan Hassell, Robert Hutchinson, Michelle Lowman, James Markham, Matthew Moodie, Jeff Olson, Jeffrey Pepper, Douglas Pundick, Ben Renow-Clarke, Dominic Shakeshaft, Gwenan Spearing, Matt Wade, Tom Welsh
Coordinating Editor: Kari Brooks-Copony
Copy Editor: Elizabeth Berry
Compositor: Kinetic Publishing Services, LLC
Indexer: Brenda Miller
Artist: Kinetic Publishing Services, LLC
Cover Designer: Anna Ishchenko

Distributed to the book trade worldwide by Springer Science+Business Media New York, 233 Spring Street, 6th Floor, New York, NY 10013. Phone 1-800-SPRINGER, fax (201) 348-4505, e-mail orders-ny@springer-sbm.com, or visit www.springeronline.com. Apress Media, LLC is a California LLC and the sole member (owner) is Springer Science + Business Media Finance Inc (SSBM Finance Inc). SSBM Finance Inc is a Delaware corporation.

For information on translations, please e-mail rights@apress.com, or visit www.apress.com.

Apress and friends of ED books may be purchased in bulk for academic, corporate, or promotional use. eBook versions and licenses are also available for most titles. For more information, reference our Special Bulk Sales–eBook Licensing web page at www.apress.com/bulk-sales.

Any source code or other supplementary materials referenced by the author in this text is available to readers at www.apress.com. For detailed information about how to locate your book's source code, go to www.apress.com/source-code/.

Contents at a Glance

Preface ix

About the Author xiii

Introduction xv

PART I ▪▪▪ Whole Consistency

CHAPTER ONE   Orientation 3

CHAPTER TWO   Bi-design 25

CHAPTER THREE Untangled Web 45

PART II ▪▪▪ Derived Simplicity

CHAPTER FOUR   x = Why 71

CHAPTER FIVE   Live and Unscripted 87

CONCLUSION 123

APPENDIX A 129

APPENDIX B 143

APPENDIX C 151

DATA-ORIENTED DICTIONARY 153

INDEX 179

Contents

Preface ix

About the Author xiii

Introduction xv

PART I ▪▪▪ Whole Consistency

▪CHAPTER ONE   Orientation 3

Some Other Ramifications 3
Related to Programming 5
Some Languages 11
Some Hardware and Software Manufacturers 20
Some Other Languages 21
Incremental Adaptation 23

▪CHAPTER TWO   Bi-design 25

Analyzing 25
Designing 28
Mechanism Characteristics 29
Network Characteristics 34
Applying Philosophy 35
Very Broad Philosophy 42
General Recommendation 44

▪CHAPTER THREE   Untangled Web 45

Overall Processing Flows 45
Keyboard-Only Interaction 45
Visual Object Interaction 49
Network Browsers 52
Just Text and Pictures 52
Added Interaction and Manageability 55

Network Site Servers 57
    More Java 57
    Storage Interaction 59
    Preprocessing for Variability. 59
    Variable Markup 60
    Storage Interaction with a New Subcontext 62
    Standardized Objects 63
    Much More Java 63
    Standardized Distributed Objects 64
Server Processing Reorganization 65
    The Foundation. 65
    Building on Management 66
    Refinement 67
    Visual Object Implementation in a New Context. 67
The Variety of Syntax 68

PART II ▨▨▨ Derived Simplicity

▨CHAPTER FOUR   x = Why

 x = Why 71
Function Set Network Representation 71
    Syntax 71
    Identification Notation. 76
    Shorthand 76
    Name Notation 77
    Common Examples 78
    Resulting General Observations 83
Database Representation. 84
    Syntax 84
    Shorthand 85
    Resulting General Observations 85
Interaction Algebra II. 85

▨CHAPTER FIVE   Live and Unscripted

 Live and Unscripted 87
More Data Orientation 87
Data Relationship Management 89
    Direct Effects on Programming 90
A Dream Language 91
Syntax of D 92
    General Formats 93
    Set Definitions 95

Fundamental Body Statement 96
Major Definitions (Header Statements) 96
Minor Definitions (Body Statements) 98
Interval Orientation 110
Aspect Orientation 115
Reserved Words 117
An Example of D 118
Possible D Design Stages 120

Conclusion 123

Reading Recommendations 124
Orientation 124
Bi-design 125
Untangled Web 126

APPENDIX A 129

Syntax of Descript 129
General Formats 129
Management Definitions 130
Major Definitions (Header Statements) 130
Body Statements 131
Interval Orientation 136
Aspect Orientation 139
Reserved Words 140

APPENDIX B 143

Syntax of Desc 143
Reserved Words 144
An Example of Desc 147

APPENDIX C 151

Procedure-Oriented to Data-Oriented Translation Key 151
Concepts 151
Keyphrases 152

DATA-ORIENTED DICTIONARY 153

INDEX 179

Preface

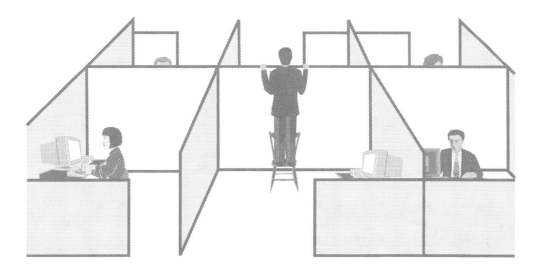

This book is directly aimed to eliminate exhausting amounts of frustration in getting to know and working with software objects in the most effective ways. It is concise and broad—and definitely *not* simplistic—specifically to strengthen each reader's object-oriented mentality and to mentally solidify individual pieces of information. This is because conciseness is more compatible with memory, and broadness is more compatible with understanding.

Very often, a book must be read once, just to get a general feeling for it; then, most or all of it must be read a second time to begin to thoroughly absorb the details. That's because each layer of the subject has been broken up into completely separate pieces of the book, which go from the most general to the most specific information for each aspect. As a result, the reader doesn't know much about the overall structure and, therefore, doesn't know how the details fit into it.

This book uses the strategy of hierarchic conveyance of information—explaining the most important components and how they relate to each other, then demonstrating how the next most important components fit with the structure that has been established, and continuing to build a solid mentality in that manner, including making recommendations for further reading for further details. With a mental structure established, the details can be taken in more individually, with the objective of directly understanding individual functionality. And the other recommended books effectively cover multiple views of the same topics; multiple views of any topic *intersect* in a strong overall feeling for it. But other books can be recommended for only Part I of this book, because Part II advances to places where no other books go.

This book is driven by the fact that *accuracy*—consistently aligned mentality—has fundamental and far-reaching benefits for beginners and veterans alike. Being accurate translates into not cutting important corners, which translates into eliminating holes at all levels of designs, causing them to flow *much* more smoothly. The end result is developers' *power* over the software. After all, the entire object-oriented concept is *based on* clarity. It's based on a flow of *thinking*. And it's the flow that provides something extra. This is a parallel to the fact that aligned molecules produce a flow of energy that provides a magnetic force.

The explanations of this book leverage both straightforward logic and significant new points of view to establish consistent orientation at all levels, eliminate bottlenecks in thinking and development, and create a *single feel* for the spectrum of object orientation. This is an example of the fact that consistency in any endeavor eliminates complication. This book was specifically written *across* concepts of object orientation, in order to establish *context* for any focus. It explains some concepts and uses some vocabulary as other explanations don't, allowing it to tie everything together as other explanations can't. Especially for a subject like this, having a clear mentality for all of its ramifications, all at the same time, is integral to real success. Without that, it's possible to make things *work*, but they're then far from optimal. Having a clear mentality frees developers to concentrate their efforts on the most effective solutions for each situation.

This book draws simple parallels between aspects of the entire development process. Its explanations make other explanations easier to understand, *explicitly* providing the cohesion and intuition that they don't. Also, it addresses explicitly points and concepts that are commonly perceived only vaguely. Further, it introduces comprehensive tools to best manage and work with object orientation; these actually further clarify the characteristics of software and its development. All of this is immediately very useful to every member of any software development team, at every level of responsibility. And the fact that it's fundamentally easier to understand and manage systems through these approaches will make them extremely valuable industrywide.

With a strong mentality, training requirements are much less of an impediment to choosing the best technology for the job at hand. The task is not about what exactly the team members (and potential team members) have done before. It's not about making the problem fit the solution. And it's not about just rolling the dice and doing what's trendy. It's about the practical ability to jump into a project and learn just the relevant details, at every level, very quickly; this is a parallel to the concept of a class structure and its extensions. More fundamentally, it applies to unobstructed mentality and directed checklists, working together to achieve optimal productivity. It's ultimately an extension of the principle that mental flexibility enables the best systems. Straightforward actions are just as helpful to developers as they are to users; further, straightforward mentality allows developers to continually and comprehensively relate to users—which enables the best systems.

Now, explaining it in one paragraph doesn't do it any kind of justice, but *iterating infusion* describes the fact that any system has multiple coexisting levels and that, repeatedly, separate but compatible technologies are brought together to create advancements. These can be baby-steps or leaps, with little more effort or even less effort. In more general terms, the same thing in a different context can take on much more power. And, actually, this phenomenon is at the heart of object-oriented software.

Organization of This Book

Iterating Infusion has a comprehensive introduction and five chapters in two parts, each feeding the next, building to the last. It is highly recommended that all be read, in order, by any audience. Skimming or skipping around is not nearly as effective. It's the entire book that demonstrates iterating infusion, a phenomenon that is independent of the subjects that are examined explicitly.

The first segment of the book, "Introduction", is crucial to the book as a whole. It's actually a set of introductions, one for each part of the book, all in one place. With this device, the course through the entire book is made immediately thoroughly familiar.

Part I, "Whole Consistency", contains the following:

- **Chapter One, Orientation: Comparisons Among Objects and Structures**, presents basic object-oriented concepts in the context of more traditional views. It addresses designing and programming properties and common language syntax—tools provided to significantly ease further study.

- **Chapter Two, Bi-design: Object-Oriented Designing Strategies**, is very much geared to a designing mind-set. It breaks down characteristics of object-oriented systems and discusses strategies for gaining control of the overall development effort.

- **Chapter Three, Untangled Web: The Evolution of an Enterprise-Level Design**, lays out a very common example of how a framework of devices and classes evolves to accommodate a specific need. It ties together the previous abstract points concretely.

Part II, "Derived Simplicity", consists of the following:

- **Chapter Four, x = Why: Interaction Algebra for Analyzing and Designing**, explains a specialized mathematically-based notation for describing object interactions. This highly structured technique helps to eliminate design holes and illuminate characteristics of object relationships, both general and specific.

- **Chapter Five, Live and Unscripted: Object Animation, a Clearer View of Automation**, establishes a revolutionarily simpler view of all software, especially object-oriented, and delineates a different *type* of software language—data oriented, as opposed to extended procedure oriented—that is derived from that view and fundamentally serves development.

Finally, the "Conclusion" element is a very brief wrap-up. It clearly demonstrates how much simpler and more advanced software development is with the understandings that the rest of the book provides.

Also, this book uses visual techniques that are specifically designed to best reinforce conveyance. First and foremost, it presents each diagram *before* the text that applies to it. This arrangement fosters mental focus, as opposed to trailing diagrams, which, ultimately, only tame scattered thoughts. Because of the common parallel, this technique is called "picture captioning". Next, the book throws a "spotlight" on key points, in a bordered box with a different font, immediately following the paragraph in which the point appears. Last, it rearranges series of related information each into a list, immediately following the paragraph in which the series appears. Additionally, it employs all of these visual attributes in shades of gray, to contrast with the black text, for extra visual dimension.

A HELPFUL REMINDER

It should be kept in mind that many books, including the titles recommended by this one, have code examples that can be fundamentally difficult to follow, in at least three ways.

First, most of them don't have any degree of explanation of the code until after it, even to explain the basic functionality of other code that the example *uses*. They unfortunately don't employ the technique of "telegraphing"—that is, explaining the basic flow of the example, then showing the code, and then explaining it in detail. An effect of this is that interpreting the code can have a lot of gaps. In reading untelegraphed code, skipping to the explanation and referencing the code along the way is the quickest way to understanding the example.

Second, many complex examples present the code in fragments, between sets of explanation text, with very little visual assistance. These fragments are from both the same class and differing classes, again with very little visual differentiation. Even something as simple as separation lines between the text and the code, and a note-font class name header for each fragment, help to make all of the parts immediately distinctive. This has an effect of losing conveyance of the organization of the code—the whole point of object orientation. The only compensation for this is reviewing the example, mentally combining the fragments in the appropriate ways.

And third, some of the examples ultimately seem functionally pointless, specifically because they use hard-coded values in places where variables make more sense. They do this, of course, to make the examples shorter—not requiring database access—but they usually don't mention it; an effect is that actual purpose is not conveyed. They could refer to variables that they explain come from an unseen database access, but they often don't. In these cases, a mental substitution of variables from a database helps to establish purpose.

About the Author

GREG ANTHONY is a near-lifelong systems analyst who has been designing and programming software since he was 8 years of age, professionally since he was 12. In over 15 years, he has worked in all areas of development and systems management, often as a consultant, in environments from PC to mid-range to mainframe, and in industries including finance, insurance, retail, and transportation.

Throughout his career, he has also created utilities of all sizes to automate development tasks, especially code generators (fourth-generation tools), code analyzers (diagnostic tools), version-control facilities, and system software interface redesigns, enabling both extreme user friendliness and extreme efficiency—in both execution and development.

He is an alumnus of the Johns Hopkins University's Center for Talented Youth, the landmark organization for gifted children 8 to 18. He has compiled interlocking philosophies mostly through independent studying and experimentation. And his ability to explain things in plain language, and in many ways, has taken him from tutoring to training to dedicated writing.

Introduction

This is a comprehensive introduction to each part of the book, preceded by a very brief history, for complete context.

A Very Brief History

Computer software development has been occurring for decades. Everyone knows that the purpose of computer software is to help them to accomplish things. Software is *applied* to a variety of tasks, processes, and methods—for example, documentation (word processing), accounting, and picture manipulation—so each of these is called an **application**.

On first thought, the best way to create an application is to arrange all of it in *one* big group, but when an application has several major tasks, it's better to break up them into multiple units (**programs**), one for each major task. Further, it seems that the best way to arrange each program is consecutively, from beginning to end; this is known as **procedural** or **fall-through** code.

But *soft*ware is fundamentally changeable, as opposed to hardware, which is fundamentally *un*changeable, or firmware, which is hardware with switches (for logical options). And software has never occurred in completely consecutive steps; that began with the basic concept of **branching**—selecting the next step based on a condition while the program is running (executing). Over time, the more flexible software needed to be, the more complex branching became, and changing an application came to require *a lot* of searching through code to figure out execution paths—the actual order of the steps.

To *manage* branching, the concept of **structuring** software came about. Most succinctly put, this grouped the steps *between the branches*, creating a *logical organization*, with each branch *referencing* a group. Further, this created **modules**, *isolated* pieces of software, and even *categorized* them, meaning that different modules could accomplish the same types of things. It reduced searching significantly, but changing an application still required making changes in multiple pieces of code to accomplish a single functional change and figuring out how to improve one function without harming another.

To manage branching *better*, and especially to manage changes, the concept of organizing the groups into *functional* units became popularized, effectively extending modularization, isolation, and categorization. These units are commonly called **objects**, and the functional grouping is commonly called **object orientation**. This organization essentially helped to *centralize* code changes and make the pieces *more independent* of each other. With it, a functional change became much more self-contained (**encapsulated**) and safe.

Whole Consistency (Part I)

The principles of object orientation have made the processes of software development simpler. But, from its most introductory teaching, the principles themselves have commonly been made too complex. Further, this has led to the exponential complexity that comes with trying to have an off-the-shelf approach to every conceivable situation; so development is again becoming more and more of an effort, instead of less and less. This is because of the overhead of extensive conformity—and the fact that required closely related code modules effectively result in just structured software with more referencing. (This is also the fundamental flaw that many structured software veterans see, causing them to stay away from newer technologies.)

The vast benefits of object-oriented software require investments of managing and working with complex designs, which include many interdependent and dynamic components. Misunderstandings, large and small, about these complexities detract from the designs' effectiveness, blatantly and esoterically. And, compared with the earlier orientations, most of the techniques of object orientation are each only a *slightly* different approach to a task, with a different name; sometimes, the name is the *only* thing that is different. But a few things are *significantly* different, and the complication is that these are what the rest fall around. Over the years, as the popularity of object orientation has spread, designers and engineers have developed many pointed strategies for improving their effectiveness. But more comprehensive—more fundamentally effective—strategies tend to elude them, and far too many projects still fail, because knowing only technical devices is not enough.

There is a growing movement to simplify—to keep systems as simple as possible, as often as possible—to minimize developmental overhead. Much the way systems have historically needed to be overhauled, at a higher level, there is a growing movement to fundamentally overhaul the world of object-oriented software and its development. This higher level of overhaul becomes more necessary because of the open nature of the industry's evolution, specifically facilitated and intensified by the self-contained changeability of object orientation, which allows one group's changes to be plugged into several others'. Very effectively, however, this higher level of overhaul incorporates the newer technology of "hot swapping", because it must be driven by mental shifting—seeing existing, functional systems in new ways. This maximizes derived practical effectiveness. (It also allows all of those structured veterans to make the leap that they haven't yet.) And understanding how the spectrum of concepts fits together allows simplification without loss of power.

Orientation: Comparisons Among Objects and Structures (Chapter One)

Forget the fancy vocabulary. Forget the structure bashing. Forget the idea that object-oriented software is completely different from structured software. It *is* different thinking, but it really just requires a *solid* overview to clearly see how they are very much the same behind the scenes. And structured software veterans can leverage what they already understand from structures.

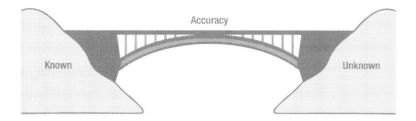

Further, there are established keywords and explanations of some aspects of object orientation that are misleading, so they unnecessarily complicate overall comprehension. For example, ambiguous meanings show a lack of accuracy: commonly in object orientation, "parent" and "child" are used to describe both object *definition* relationships and object collection relationships, and these relationships entail very different things. Most directly here, instead of the *leap* that is commonly required to get the feeling of object orientation, accuracy provides an easy bridge. This book delineates both the standard and more accurate vocabularies, so whenever the standard words are misleading, the more accurate words can simply be mentally substituted.

Sometimes, differing words for the same thing are reasonably driven by differing points of view—differing contexts. In fact, the history of software has had *many* instances of one entity being seen in multiple ways. Among many other benefits, being able to understand everything from a consistent point of view eliminates the frequent need for extra effort at figuring out context.

And two things should be kept in mind:

- *Procedure* orientation was the *pre*structured orientation.

- The structured software development process has created a great deal of excellent software.

Related to Designing

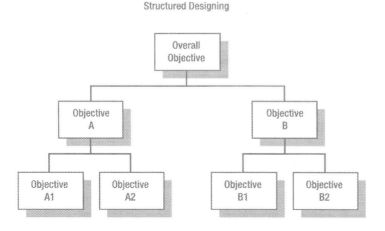

The first thing that is needed in this overview is a comparable overview of the structured software development process. Ultimately, the structured process requires a system analysis that arrives at a design of **a hierarchic structure of objectives,** from the most general to the most specific. At all levels, this defines data items and what happens to them (processes). With each level of the hierarchy ordered chronologically, the system functions are clear. At that point, scenarios (also known as **use cases**) can be run through the structure, chaining the components in execution sequence, as a cross-check to make sure that nothing is missed. The structure also directly accommodates data flow diagrams (and process flow diagrams, which aren't really necessary when data flow diagrams are geared to low-enough levels of the system structure—but that's a later subject). It even includes the code-level objectives; structured programs are contiguous subsets of the overall system structure. Common functions are usually repeated and tailored to each particular usage.

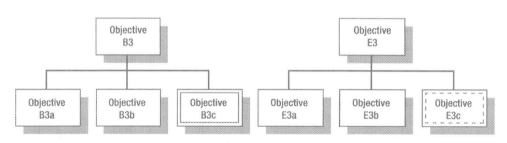

Similarities and Differences

B3c and E3c differ.

The object-oriented software development process requires a system analysis that arrives at a design of **a network of *sets* of objectives.** This puts more focus on the functions than just how they fit into the system. The object-oriented process actually can continue from the point of the scenarios running through the structure. *Objects are defined by the similarities and differences between the execution scenarios.* This includes varying degrees of likely future scenarios, both common and system-specific. The combinations of similarities and differences define how code can be shared. A parallel to this can be found with conditional combinations—"and" and "or" conditions, sometimes with multiple sets of parentheses, in an "if" test—in their separation into progressing segments—with individual tests. Objects can then be further separated by whether shared segments are (very) closely related.

Of course, there are very different ways of looking at the object-oriented development process, especially as familiarity brings feeling for objects. Other views prove to be more direct, but this one can always serve as context for them. Universally, the most critical skill, in *any* orientation, is the ability to recognize patterns—commonalities, differentiations, and *dependencies.*

Taking a good look, it can be seen that *any application of an object-oriented network still requires the structured linking of objects;* in other words, the practical usage of object orientation still fundamentally requires an aspect of structured development. In many cases, no code, in any form, is written without an application in mind; there, at the very least, code can be created more independently than in pure structured development. This even allows *pieces* of systemwide functionality to be explicitly coded. Before this approach, the only way to handle pieces of functionality was with standard methods (protocols). Ultimately, object orientation is a very thorough way of approaching the traditional separation of shared code into utility programs.

The well-known idea of software objects is that they model objects that physically exist in the real world. Their data and processes are seen to be *characteristics*. But one reality of software objects is that they can also model objects that don't (yet) physically exist in the real world; these are conceptual objects. Looking at that more broadly, every built object that does physically exist was a conceptual object first; in other words, every physical object was a mental object first. And, often, there's no justification for building the physical object; but software is more flexible. This includes that a conceptual object can be shared with—in other words, implicitly duplicated for—other objects.

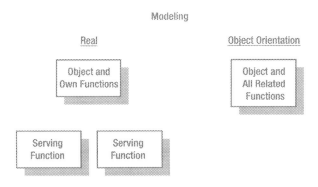

However, in an even more fundamental way, each object isn't really based on a real object; it's more based on functions that a real object *needs*. The significant practical difference between the two concepts is that interobject checks and balances are needed in the real world because of the factor of a lack of object integrity, but this factor doesn't exist in software. A very good example is that, in the real world, an employee can't be relied on to do his or her own payroll with complete integrity, but this is a perfect function to have in an employee object, simply because it serves the employee. This understanding is commonly utilized but not much mentioned. Commonly, a description of a particular class is that it "represents" a particular real object; here, it can be helpful to mentally substitute the word "serves".

Bi-design: Object-Oriented Designing Strategies (Chapter Two)

The inanimate components of any field of designing can have characteristics of being alive. The most effective designing requires feeling that phenomenon. It requires deeply understanding the components, individually and collectively, and balancing all of their needs at the same time; it requires orchestration. And it requires a *dedicated* thought process. As they are in many things, simple philosophies are the best guide through all levels of designing. Also, the biggest reason why there is a gap between cutting-edge (research-developed) designing techniques and everyday (business-practiced) ones is that the organization and length of common teaching techniques make it too difficult both to see the thinking that drives a comprehensive process and to understand how to apply it. This results in an inability to *manage* the process. What's needed is a comprehensive set of simple object-oriented designing philosophies and a dynamic overall strategy for applying them in various situations.

Interaction Mechanisms

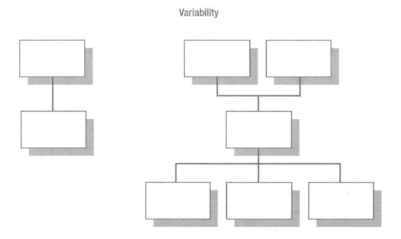

Initial development requires creation of a network of classes *before* they can be combined to create an application, although third-party sets can be acquired and tailored for common functions. Combining sets to more easily create multiple applications requires areas of flexibility. The degree of flexibility that any part of the software must have has a direct impact on how complex its interaction mechanisms must be. Simply put, flexibility is served by a mechanism of variability. This is where objects (and polymorphism) contribute; they are used, in essence, as network variables—logically replacing hard-coded conditionals. This entails some factor of separation (**indirection**) between interacting methods, which is **loose coupling**, instead of **tight coupling**. The mechanism acts as a *translator*, typically between parts of the class's implementation or between its interface and its implementation.

A very simple example of indirection and loose coupling is a mathematical one. It's possible to programmatically convert a number from any base to any other base by converting to and from a constant base. For example, instead of converting directly from base 2 (binary) to base 16 (hexadecimal), converting from base 2 to base 10 (decimal), and then base 10 to base 16, yields the same result. And, with this configuration, any beginning and ending bases are possible with no further programming. (Because letters are used for digit values above 9, the highest practical base is 36—10 numerals + 26 letters.) This concept also relates to the properties of probabilities: the possible permutations—combinations considering sequence—of two factors are the possibilities of each, multiplied by the other; being able to deal with them separately is usually much less overall work. It's also why digital (representative individualized) processing has much more power than analog (quantitative overall) processing.

These loosely coupled parts are each a *type* of class (or part of a class); they each specialize in a particular type of role. This understanding brings object-oriented designing up another level. It's then fairly easy to see how individual parts of the same type can be swapped for each other, and how a team (an interdependent collection) of types of parts can be needed to build a whole logical function. While a usage of loose coupling is more difficult to comprehend, a usage of tight coupling is more difficult to change. Tight coupling means that parts are directly dependent on each other, which means that changes in one part are more likely to adversely affect other parts and thus require more changes. So, tight coupling (direct dependence) cascades the effects of changes.

It's very enlightening, here, to take a look at a bit of software history. When there was very little memory available for any one program, programs were very restricted in size; each was, therefore, a functional module. As memory availability grew, so did programs; few developers recognized the value of the interdependent pieces of code. The most popular thing to do was the easier thing, which didn't include the extra considerations of the ability to directly swap one piece of code for another; consequently, *the inherent modularity was lost*. It can easily be seen that those extra considerations at that time could have caused object orientation to become popular much earlier in software's history; it can easily be seen that the trends of software designing might actually have just gone in the wrong direction at that time.

Across all of the object-oriented systems that have ever existed, all of the countless interaction mechanisms have been of only a relatively few types; all of the interaction mechanisms of any particular type have common characteristics (components and behaviors). These types are commonly known as **design patterns**, and learning them makes designing simpler and smoother. Ultimately, they are standardized techniques for manipulating interaction variables. But it should be clearly understood that these are *design* patterns, not design*ing* patterns, which are part of what are commonly known as methodologies. A pattern of designing *needs* and ways to serve them defines a designing pattern (which includes an analyzing phase). There are many designing patterns, from many sources, public and private—and the public designing patterns must be tailored to best serve each (private) environment.

Software creation requires iterations of analyzing, then designing, and then programming (which is really the lowest level designing). The best software design creation requires thorough understanding of all of the levels and how to best manage them. To clarify how the various types of mechanisms fit together, it's very helpful to understand that interaction *types* need to be *identified* in the *analyzing* efforts, and interaction *mechanisms* need to be *applied* in the *designing* efforts. Ultimately, the best software design creation requires being able to *feel* the mechanisms.

Ultimately, design patterns are standardized techniques for manipulating interaction variables.

At a higher level, having a feel for combinations of all of these things, in combinations of circumstances, determines designing *strategies*.

Untangled Web: The Evolution of an Enterprise-Level Design (Chapter Three)

The open nature of the industry's evolution continually allows the better ideas to be built on—sometimes directly, sometimes only logically (through the lessons learned from them)—and to often gain popularity—which then feeds good ideas, and so on. This is based on ongoing occurrences of practical usage, adjustments for deficiencies, discussions and judgments, and comparisons of effectiveness. Overall, it fosters the best designs.

All software applications have the same basic characteristics. Most basically, to help people accomplish things, an application must interact with its users, manipulate information for them, and save relevant information for later usage. The common **3-tier architecture** design is of user presentation, core logic, and data storage. The separation of these most-basic functions is another example of serving flexibility.

Applications have always required ways to communicate with their users. The avenues for this, and the methods for managing them, have expanded and become much more effective over the years. The mouse has become very familiar, with the abilities that it provides to point and click, drag and drop, and scroll. Before these were only the abilities to type commands and fill in the blanks, with the keyboard.

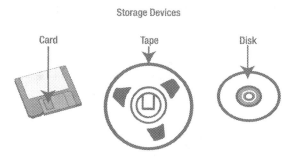

Applications have also always required ways to store data for later usage. These avenues and their management have likewise, independently, expanded and become much more effective. Hardware for this has built from cards, to paper tape, to magnetic tape, to magnetic disk—logically, a tape roll turned on its side—to optical (laser-based) disk; these have increased storage density, and practical capacity, all along the way. Cards could accommodate only fixed-length records; beginning with tapes, variable-length records were possible. The only storage method possible until disks came about was sequentially accessed files. Disks enabled indexed (effectively randomly accessed) files and databases, which are combinations of indexed logical files. (They can be physical files, but databases are most efficiently managed as physical partitions of a single file.)

And, of course, applications have always been mostly thought of as what they do. At their heart, their processing is various calculations—comparisons, searches, extractions, duplications—and combinations of all of these. The basic functions have always been the same. But the ever-increasing speed of *hard*ware and the ever-increasing flexibility of techniques continue to make more and more applications practical.

Also independently, only relatively recently have the client/server and added internet concepts come about and become widespread.

Early on, there was one user interface per computer; it was very similar to a typewriter, so the interaction was one line at a time. This interface could be shared by multiple users, taking turns. Eventually, the interface became a screen, but the interaction was still by single line. The idea of multiple interfaces per computer was made possible by the idea that the computer would give each interface a turn; so, many screens were *part of* one central computer.

OPERATING SYSTEMS

Computers have long separated more computer-dedicated operations and more user-dedicated applications with an **operating system** (**OS**). There have been and are many operating systems. An OS is actually just a set of programs—some of which the computer is always running. An OS has one main program, the **kernel**, and several extension programs, **system programs**, that the kernel runs only when needed.

The simplest explanation of how the kernel gets running is that, when the computer is turned on, it looks at a constant location on its startup disk—the **boot sector**—for the variable location of the OS kernel and starts it. Applications are started as requested by the user, immediately or by schedule, and effectively further extend the OS. Giving each interface a turn is a function of the OS.

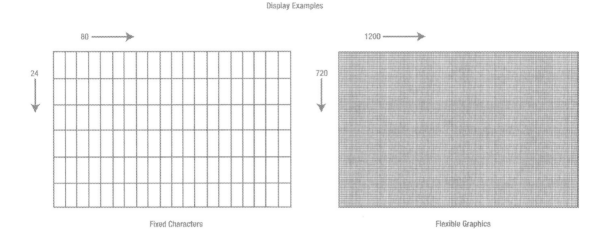

Also, user interfaces grew to include a degree of formatting. Each of the positions on each of the lines of the screen became identified by its coordinates, so many pieces of information could be addressed in one interface. Eventually, a **graphical user interface** (**GUI**) was made possible through the much finer coordinates of picture elements (**pixels**).

Early on, computers were *huge*—taking up to entire warehouses. Over time, multiple-user computers became *much* smaller, even as they became much more powerful. Again independently, the idea of one user interface per *very* small (personal) computer grew; over time, these computers went from having very little power to having more power than the warehouse-sized computers of decades earlier. Their growing capabilities spawned the idea of making the large computers even more powerful by using them in place of screens and shifting some of the overall processing to them. So, each of the small computers became a *client* of a large computer, which became a *server* of the application. Most directly, the client and the server are not the computers but corresponding *software* on the computers.

The client and the server are software.

Eventually came the idea of connecting servers, to form a *network*; this *distributed* processing and storage among many computers. Later came the idea of connecting networks, to form the *internet*. By comparison, this made an unconnected network an internal network, or int*r*anet. The internet has both public and private networks; a public subset of the internet, the **World Wide Web** (**WWW**), is commonly *referred to* as the internet or "the web". Then, another version of both mouse and keyboard client interfaces, the network browser, even gave the internet (and intranets) interaction capabilities that weren't available through any other configuration. Although networks can transmit any types of files, the web is commonly thought of in the context of *viewing* through a browser.

The 3-tier design can be applied on a single computer or a client/server configuration, using the client for the presentation tier and the server for the core (middle) tier and the storage tier. The storage tier can even have a separate server, to shift some heavy processing; this is a level of indirection. (In a context focused on the core/storage relationship, the software that manages the usage of this type of server has been called **middleware**.) A computer that is used as a server can actually have an application that has existed for a long time—a **legacy** system—and *might* still have users.

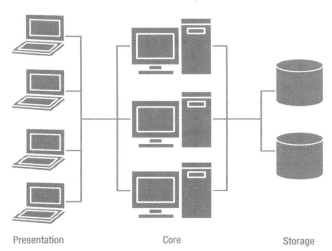

n-Node 3-Tier Configuration

Presentation   Core   Storage

Further, there can be *multiple* storage servers. That configuration can even be used for multiple legacy systems, effectively combined by the core tier. Even further, the design can be applied to distributed processing, as multiple *core* servers. So, a single tier can have many instances; this is commonly called **n-tier**, but it's still the 3-tier design, just with *n* nodes. The term **enterprise software** refers to an application for shared data, typically among employees of a company; this can actually be applied to any shared configuration, but the term was created for the 3-tier design on the client/server configuration, because of its complexity.

Occurring at the same time as object orientation, and adding to its uses, all of these technologies are also becoming more organized—and more extensive. The newer ones have increasing infrastructure, fairly standardized, built by relatively few organizations. While this significantly intensifies each learning curve, at the same time, it allows designers and programmers to have more and more examples of (usually) very solid software to study and, to varying degrees, pattern after, because the infrastructures are built by experts—developers who are closest to the origin of the technologies or developers who have specific insights. So, this aspect is a compensation; it diminishes the learning curve.

Increasing infrastructure both intensifies and diminishes each learning curve.

The open nature of the industry defines the industry as a whole as the *collection* of experts. On the other hand, the occurrences of lack of simple philosophy throughout the industry cause this expertise to not be distributed as thoroughly as possible. Further, they cause varying degrees of confusion—which then feeds errors being built on errors. But understanding the various aspects of each design, and how the designs are related, cuts through both of these issues.

For complete context, for a fundamentally thorough demonstration of examples of designing and programming, and to serve simple philosophies, it's very important to understand how user and storage interfaces have been implemented in various hardware and software configurations—and the reasons behind the design decisions. And it's especially important to examine how the later approaches were built on the older ones, sometimes directly, sometimes only logically.

Then, all of this provides strong feeling for possibilities.

Derived Simplicity (Part II)

Structured software is very application specific. Object-oriented software is less application specific and very function specific. In fact, structured software could comparably be called **application oriented**. And, looking deeper, objects are actually *logical sets of functions*; object-oriented software could, more completely, be called "function-set oriented" or, more fundamentally, **function oriented**. (Calling the software function oriented is the subject of some debate, because objects have data outside of functions also, but these are separated into function sets by *functionality* and shared by the functions and separate executions of the same function.) And each complex logical function is still structured, in multiple code functions. For conceptual clarity (and fundamental benefits throughout the concepts), function orientation is the name that is generally used in this book.

Structured software could comparably be called "application oriented". And object-oriented software could, more fundamentally, be called "function oriented"; each function is still structured.

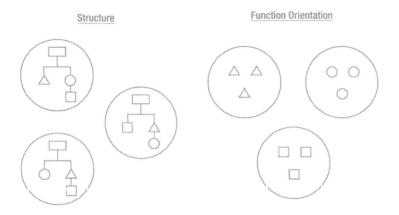

Function-oriented thinking sees application-oriented thinking as fragmenting logical sets of functions and, additionally, unnecessarily duplicating many of those fragments. Without the duplication of fragments, each function—data and processing—is *owned* by a set; other sets must interact with that set to use the function. Developers must know what parameters each function requires and what *all* of its *external effects* are; but this has always been true of utilities. (And, actually, the best designs *separate* any side effect into its own function, allowing selective combination.) The most organized function-oriented approach is to have a database of the functions with "uses" and "is used by" references— as part of an integrated development environment (IDE). These added efforts allow each logical function to occur physically only once, so changes are centralized—and distributed by the computer; ongoing development is facilitated, so the added efforts are an investment in the future.

The main point of function orientation is easing of the ongoing development effort.

Functions *are* the heart of applications, so building *multiple* applications is more *organized* with a well-organized function set network (as is changing a single application). The key is that each set needs to be well defined, because poorly defined sets actually make changing them more complex. This means that each set should have a cohesive *purpose*, and a fairly limited one. A good guide is that a piece of code that benefits from a comment can actually be separated into its own function, or even its own function set, with a name that serves as the comment. A very straightforward example is that input and output for a particular record type should be in a dedicated set; these create what are known as **data objects**. It can be seen that when sets are too large, the structure of the functions dominates the network of the sets—so the system is actually application oriented.

Whereas application-oriented sets perform deep processing on a narrow spectrum of data, function-oriented sets perform shallow processing on a wide spectrum of data. In fact, to application-oriented veterans, function-oriented code can look unreasonably simplistic, so its jumping from module to module can seem pointless. But the limited purpose promotes function independence and, therefore, code swapability; this allows more possible recombinations of sets and, therefore, more possible applications, so that no application is overcommitted. An advantage of a whole logical function over just pieces of application-oriented code is that it is a complete unit; it ensures operational integrity. The ideal for building multiple applications is for there to be very little new design necessary for each new application; that would be like prefabricated development (with adjustable components). That's the whole idea: there's no *magic* in objects.

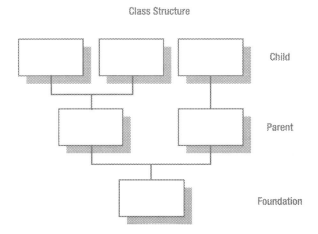

Class Structure

Child

Parent

Foundation

For perspective, it is very important to remember that both application-oriented and function-oriented systems are only logical views of a system. *The actual system occurs at execution, in a sequence, and that is essentially the same for both.* (This understanding is also very important for debugging and optimizing efforts.) Additional perspective requires some design-level vocabulary. It includes understanding that the word "object" is less-frequently appropriate in function-oriented development than the word "class". (This overusage is partly a product of overfocus on "object" orientation.) A class defines an object; it's a classification. So, mostly, a class is a function set in its definition form, and an object is a function set in its usage form. Further, in various ways, a class is thought of internally, and an object is thought of externally. Any object—real-world or software—can easily be *represented* by another object—a symbol or a piece of code—but that's external; that object is still *served* by the internal.

Both application-oriented and function-oriented systems are only logical views of a system. The actual system occurs at execution, in a sequence, and that is the same for both.

Now, a class structure is commonly referred to as a hierarchy, but it isn't really a hierarchy. In that representation, the higher levels wouldn't manage the lower levels; in fact, the reverse would be true. The clearest representation of a class structure is a literal *tree* structure (an upside-down hierarchy), which denotes that descendants are built on top of ancestors; descendants are more defined. Actually, the tree structure points out that they are really *a*scendants; this is a word that will be used from here on. A tree and a hierarchy (a near-literal *pyramid*, or a literal *root* structure) are mirror images, so they have a lot in common, and that causes confusion between them, but it's fundamentally important to understand the differences—and their effects. A child class is commonly referred to as a **subclass**, and a parent class is commonly referred to as a **superclass**, but these names, again, are compatible with a hierarchy. (Just to check the thinking, standard set theory can look at sets from two different points of view: abstract [from above] and concrete [from the side]. It's the abstract view, which serves theorization [digging to foundations], that says that a variable encompasses all of its constants. The concrete view, which serves application [building functionality], says that a superset has all of the characteristics of its subsets. A class structure is analyzed from the top and viewed from the side.) Each class structure can simply be called a **family**, and each class has a **lineage**. Other appropriate terminology refers to a parent as an **extended** class and a child as an **extension** class. Also appropriate, extending can be referred to as **specializing** or **growing**. The structure of a class and its ascendants is a **branch**; alternately, a descendant (ancestor) can be seen as a **platter** (or platform) for its ascendants. It's important to note that this is a static system, because each child can be in only one part of the family at a time. Further, it's a *doubly* static system, because each child can be in only one part of the family *ever*.

A very important point (which is very rarely made) is that, with one exception, *any one object is defined by more than one class*. The common explanation is as follows. An object is an **instance** of a class; the declaration of an object is an **instantiation**. Any class can be a parent class and have further definition in its child class, which **inherits** its parts (data items and functions); this includes that functions can be *re*defined. (The fact that, in the real world, a child is born of two parents can be supported also. The other parent is most appropriately identified as a step of the designing process.) But the accurate explanation of instantiation further accounts for the fact that each class inherits its parts; each object is an instance of its *lineage* (a class and all of its ancestors). In some environments, there is a most-basic generic class, which all other classes ascend from; any object of this class is the only type that has a lineage of just one class.

x = Why: Interaction Algebra for Analyzing and Designing (Chapter Four)

Beyond class network characteristics—from family structures to individual functions—the cooperative processes between classes in function-oriented systems can be very cumbersome and (therefore) difficult to communicate from one developer to another. So, comfort with a design among a team of developers (of all levels) spreads slowly—and discomfort (of varying degrees) lingers for the life of the system. This is a fundamental disabling factor in initial and continuing development. But it doesn't have to be.

It's frequently valuable to convey information with visual organization. Commonly, it's believed that text cannot be organized very visually and that the best way to present information visually is with diagrams. Specifically, for cooperative processes in function-oriented systems, the Unified Modeling Language (UML), especially its "structure" and "sequence" diagrams, is popular. Some problems with diagrams, however, are that they often take more space than text for the amount of information that they contain, and they are comparatively time-consuming to produce well.

Of course, text *can* be organized visually, in many ways. Further, when it's possible, the most efficient way to convey information visually is with mathematical notations. And an important part of the simplification movement is minimization of separate documentation effort.

An extremely clarifying view of class interaction mechanisms comes from a very structured, very concise technique for analyzing interactions and designing mechanisms, with a notation called **interaction algebra**. This concept grew out of the fact that there are several common characteristics between interaction mechanisms and standard algebra, including core manipulation concepts.

The first obvious commonality is the fact that, in both, flexibility is served by a mechanism of variability; in both, this adds a level of complexity. Further, the interaction algebra notation serves to identify the user of the mechanism, just as algebra isolates a variable. Interaction algebra can be seen as an inheritance (an extension) of algebra, and the properties of the notation show themselves to be so straightforward as to clearly apply to databases (data table interactions) as well.

Design Holes

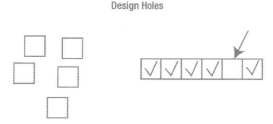

The fact that interaction algebra is oriented to the user of any mechanism focuses attention on the *purpose* of the mechanism, which is an extremely important factor for analyzing and designing, especially as it applies to classes and their interactions. And a fundamentally important feature of interaction algebra is that, as with any structured approach, it eliminates design holes that free-form representations let slip by.

Interaction algebra is based on equations, just as is standard algebra. But it's geared to software entity interaction mechanisms; it has a specific format for its expressions. Further, it has two sets of syntax: one to represent classes and the other to represent database tables.

Live and Unscripted: Object Animation, a Clearer View of Automation (Chapter Five)

Even function orientation is a design that doesn't address the largest aspect of automation. Aside from the orientation to structures or functions, systems can be oriented to processes or data. In that larger context, function orientation, in its common form, is really a function-oriented procedure design. And, of course, common function-oriented languages are extended **procedure-oriented** languages. This is because each step of any process is commonly seen as procedural.

Inside of each function, code is mostly procedure oriented. The simple concept of a function set is geared to answering the "whats" of a system, ultimately thought of as a set of data. Digging deeper, the function set's role (responsibilities) in the system must be well understood; this is geared to answering the "hows" of the system, ultimately thought of as the functions that *support the data*. So, ultimately, the data is the priority of function orientation. But the code—the procedure-oriented code—becomes more geared to answering the hows than the whats, making the procedure the priority. This causes a conflict.

In software development, designing is more from the users' point of view, to get the computer to serve *what* the users need. With procedure orientation, programming has been more from the computer's point of view, to serve the computer also. Complete software development has always required thinking in both directions at once. This is a huge complication and, therefore, a huge bottleneck in the software development timeline. But it doesn't have to be.

Of course, function orientation is designed to ease the software development effort, but the problem is, in essence, that function orientation goes only halfway. And, generically, going halfway often causes complications and extra efforts. Extending the function-oriented design to include the **data-oriented** equivalent of functions, which continue to address *the whats and then the hows* of a system, completes the concept. (For now, it's simpler to continue to call the entities functions.) With a function-oriented *data* design, the flow of thought both outside and inside of sets is in the same direction.

Data Orientation

Simply put, each system exists for a reason—more accurately, a set of reasons. This fact easily translates to the fact that any system is geared to whats—individually or in combination; that's the system as a whole and, with the complete concept of function orientation, at any level. Even each function set exists for a set of reasons.

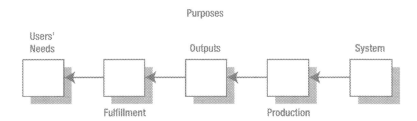

Thinking this through, the reasons why any system really exists are to produce its outputs, which are whats. This isn't *all* of its outputs, because some of them are an intermediate form to facilitate further functions, but the purposes of any system are to produce its outputs. This reinforces the fact that data orientation is more important than procedure orientation. And the **product** is the focus of data orientation.

So, data orientation isn't about just *any* data, because a system has goals—to produce its products, and data orientation is about data that is the focus, or *subject*, of each step along the way. It could also be called "product orientation", which can be derived to "purpose orientation" or, further, to "goal orientation". Or it could be seen, probably controversially, but definitely ironically, as "*sub*ject orientation". But the most straightforward and comprehensive name is data orientation.

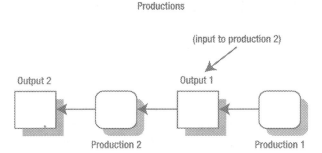

Of course, the system's inputs are important. Ultimately, a system produces all of its outputs from its inputs. More directly, the system produces some of its outputs from intermediate outputs. Really, system inputs are one form of intermediate outputs. This fact is made clear by the understanding that any system input was an output of another system (or a person). In data orientation, an input is seen as a **resource**.

The necessary derivative of focus on the products of a system is focus on the items that are necessary to assemble them—their **components**. For several years already, fourth-generation and CASE tools have commonly handled outputs in a data-oriented manner, with lists of components and their characteristics. It's extremely helpful to be able to extend that handling to account for value changes, but the limiting factor is that the value changes seldom occur in the order of the components of the output, so this aspect of these tools still requires coding and, therefore, (awkwardly) has still been procedure oriented. A data-oriented language enables this extension.

Value changes seldom occur in the order of the components of the output, so they have always been procedure oriented.

Effects on Development

The most far-reaching effect of data orientation is the fact that it allows a single mind-set throughout the entire development process. It keeps focus on all of the possible components of the system, at any level; the conditions under which each component is created are secondary to that. This focus drives development, making all efforts clearer and bringing all pieces together with less effort.

Data orientation keeps focus on all of the possible components of the system, at any level. The conditions under which each component is created are secondary to that.

Effectively, the process of software development becomes much more like the process of *idea* development. *This effort is fundamentally more natural and intuitive.*

By the way, because testing is oriented to system purposes, data orientation even facilitates that. No longer is it necessary for developers to shift gears again, to change mental direction, to flip back to the other side of the development coin.

The simplification of the development process is completed with a data-oriented *programming* language, which creates an even more extensive philosophy. Ultimately, the computer then interacts completely from *any* user's point of view; software developers are users (of software development software), and programs are these users' specifications.

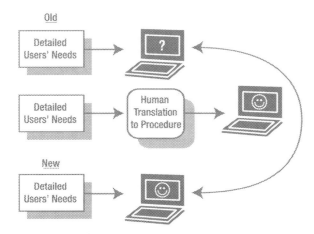

Data-oriented translators simply translate specifications that come from a different point of view. This philosophy elevates the concept of the intelligence of computers. It makes procedure-oriented computers seem dumb by comparison. The dumb computer is just a (processing) servant; the smart computer is a (data analyzing) partner and then a servant.

Whether for designing or for programming, the heart of a data-oriented language is the specification of how related pieces of data interact with each other, in the proper sequence. This task is most simply described as **data relationship management**, or **DRM**, most easily pronounced "dream". And a DRM language is made possible through a few observations about procedure-oriented languages, built on all of the observations of the earlier parts of this book.

With a strong understanding of function orientation, DRM languages are easy to adapt to. They have nearly all of the same components as function orientation, with added capabilities, so it's easy to feel the reorganization.

PART I

Whole Consistency

The first part beyond common views of software presents the range of effects of singular feeling. It specifically ties together many levels of common details, working from how concepts can be applied, individually, to how they have been applied, collectively.

■ ■ ■

CHAPTER ONE

Orientation
Comparisons Among Objects and Structures

This chapter presents several important concepts, old and new, geared to common programming languages.

Some Other Ramifications

In addition to those delineated in the Introduction, another mechanism that goes into the definition of a class is **composition**, which means that that class has a collection of parts, any of which can have a collection of other parts. A composition structure is, therefore, a true hierarchy. Also, this is a dynamic system, because each piece can be a part of multiple collections. Comparing the two, inheritance and composition are both one class's usage of another class (and composition can even be one class's recursive usage of itself), but composition requires instantiation of the used class; in other words, it requires an object. This means that inheritance allows modification of the used class (in that usage), but composition does not. It means that inheritance is an open usage, while composition is a closed usage; it means that inheritance uses a class as a "white box", and composition uses it as a "black box". (More abstractly, it's like inheritance opens a class for update, and composition opens it read-only.) But composition also "wraps" its used classes in functionality, allowing for a reasonable degree of functional modification, without the compound static restrictions of inheritance. In the class structure sense, a "wrapper" is just an added layer. By the way, the fact that composition is a hierarchy is a direct clue to the fact that that aspect of function orientation is actually still application oriented.

Whole-Functions Flows

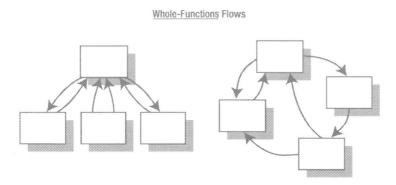

Again, function orientation produces more of a network than a structure. The standard approach to managing the network is to have a huge diagram with arrows everywhere to indicate relationships among the function sets and, further, the individual functions of those sets. This approach has a high learning curve. Ironically, the network of sets of functions is similar to a *procedure*-oriented problem: the network of commands that defined "spaghetti code". Of course, the function-oriented version of the problem is of a much lower occurrence.

Another approach that can be very helpful for a given application, immediately and on an ongoing basis, is to map the important functions onto the application structure. In other words, this mapping shows how the function sets are applied to a particular application, to serve as an example. It is a view of the function sets as application oriented. Function orientation is geared to "what", then "how"; application orientation is geared to "why", which is actually a combination of whats.

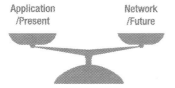

Application   Network
/Present   /Future

Decision making in the application-oriented software development process requires a feeling for the characteristics of individualized functions (in general) and their interrelationships, and has a particular balance of many factors. The complexity makes good application-oriented development an art. Likewise, decision making in the function-oriented software development process requires a feeling for the characteristics of sets (of functions) and their interrelationships, and has its own balance of many factors. Good function-oriented development is a different art. The most significant difference is that function-oriented designing must also accommodate an application; in other words, function-oriented designing is bidirectional—and that is also its most significant balance. The difference that adds the most complexity is that set interrelationships are more intensive than individualized ones. To address this, function-oriented interaction mechanisms are more sophisticated than application-oriented ones.

Set interrelationships are more intensive than individualized ones; to address this, function-oriented interaction mechanisms are more sophisticated than application-oriented ones.

Related to Programming

Much of function orientation could actually be accomplished with traditional structure-oriented languages; "traditional" means, especially, "nonblock"—languages with which every data item exists for the entire execution of the program. Block languages can have data items that exist in just a "block" of code; this grouping of data and processing already encompasses a function-oriented concept.

COMPILERS AND RUN-TIME SYSTEMS

Applications can be coded in various programming languages. A language is typically created to address programmers' needs from a specific point of view. To support the point of view, when the programming code is *translated* to computer (**machine**) **code**, it's automatically infused with some standard code, tailored to the program; so the overall process is *compiling*.

Also to support the point of view, and to eliminate repetition, some other standard code—for *services*, which aren't tailored to each program—is kept in a set of programs called a **run-time system** (**RTS**), which is used by the program automatically as it runs. Of course, both of these approaches, together with the operating system, allow programmers to focus more on the applications.

The big draw with function-oriented languages is that the compiler takes care of a lot of things that programmers have had to do manually. Modules could always be separate programs, thereby always grouping data and process definitions. Code could always be copied and portions rewritten with comments that indicate the differences. Programs could always be written from skeletons. And links could always be dynamic (variable-based).

Function-oriented compilers handle code in a more integrated way. They are, therefore, comparatively grand in scope; simply put, they operate up a level. With them, designers and programmers *think* up a level. It's easier to learn any (or all) of them first understanding reasons for its parts. The code-level vocabulary is as follows.

Based on Intermediate (Block) Languages: The establishing definitions seem obvious. An intermediate-language function is a function-oriented **method**. A program is a **class**.

- A call from one function to another is a **message**.

- The fact that a program needs operational integrity in both data and processes is **encapsulation**.

- Each occurrence of data or functions is a **member (of the class)**.

- The functional scope of a program (class) is its **granularity**.

- A program can be implicitly copied in its **derived class**—the copy is hidden—and any function can be rewritten (**overridden**).

- A copied program is a **base class**.

- The process of implicitly copying is **inheritance**.

- A program template is an **abstract class**; comparably, a program is a **concrete class**.

- Declaration of usage of one program in another is a logical **object**. (Actual objects exist only at execution—except for something like a file, which is a **persistent object**.)

- An executing program's exact combination of data (values) is its **state**.

- A set of programs is a **library** or **package**.

- The format of a call is the called function's **signature**.

- A program's collection of call formats is its **interface**.

- The program's way of handling calls is its **implementation**.

- The ability of more than one program to handle a particular call format is **polymorphism**.

- When a program's function name is used for more than one call format, that is **overloading (the method)**.

These translations are spotlighted in Table 1-1.

Table 1-1. *Block Language Vocabulary*

Block	Function Orientation
Function	Method
Program	Class
Function call	Message
Operational integrity	Encapsulation
Data item or function	Member
Functional scope	Granularity
Implicitly copied program	Derived class
Rewritten	Overridden
Copied program	Base class
Implicitly copying	Inheritance
Program template	Abstract class
Program	Concrete class
Usage of one program in another	Object
File	Persistent object
Data values	State
Set of programs	Library, package
Function's call format	Signature
Set of call formats	Interface
Call handling process	Implementation
Individualized call handling processes	Polymorphism
Function name with multiple call formats	Overloading

Based on Structure-oriented (Nonblock) Languages: These definitions are not as straightforward. For most of them, "function" is substituted with "program", and, separately, "program" is substituted with "library".

- A structured program is a function-oriented **method (of handling data)**.

- A set of programs—a *limited-purpose library*—is a **class**.

- A call from one program to another is a **message**.

- The fact that a library needs operational integrity in both data and processes is **encapsulation**.

- Each occurrence of data or programs is a **member (of the class)**.

- The functional scope of a library is its **granularity**.

- A library can be implicitly copied in its **derived class**—the copy is hidden—and any program can be rewritten (**overridden**).

- A copied library is a **base class**.

- The process of implicitly copying is **inheritance**.

- A library template is an **abstract class**; comparably, a library is a **concrete class**.

- Declaration of usage of one library in another is a logical **object**. (Actual objects exist only at execution—except for something like a file, which is a **persistent object**.)

- An executing library's exact combination of data (values) is its **state**.

- A set of (structure-oriented) libraries is a (function-oriented) **library** or **package**; this is the most succinct example of the comparative grandness of function-oriented languages.

- The format of a call is the called program's **signature**.

- A library's collection of call formats is its **interface**.

- The library's way of handling calls is its **implementation**.

- The ability of more than one library to handle a particular call format is **polymorphism**.

- When a library's program name is used for more than one call format, that is **overloading (the method)**.

These translations are spotlighted in Table 1-2.

Table 1-2. *Nonblock Language Vocabulary*

Block	Function Orientation
Program	Method
Library	Class
Program call	Message
Operational integrity	Encapsulation
Data item or program	Member
Functional scope	Granularity

Block	Function Orientation
Implicitly copied library	Derived class
Rewritten	Overridden
Copied library	Base class
Implicitly copying	Inheritance
Library template	Abstract class
Library	Concrete class
Usage of one library in another	Object
File	Persistent object
Data values	State
Set of libraries	Library, package
Program's call format	Signature
Set of call formats	Interface
Call handling process	Implementation
Individualized call handling processes	Polymorphism
Program name with multiple call formats	Overloading

The idea of encapsulation is extended to include the direct usability of a class's data and processes by other classes. (Code accessibility by developers is a different issue.) The practical power of encapsulation is that it functionally separates interfaces from implementations. With limited scoping, each function produces a product, fulfilling a set of objectives in its production. The product can be what the function returns to the caller; or it can be an effect on the system, with the function returning a notation about that effect or not returning anything. When functions are designed well (without side effects), developers mostly don't need to think about how the functions fulfill their objectives; they need to think only about how to use those functions. From the providers' side, one basic implementation can have multiple interfaces; this is actually a parallel to class specializing, or even mental directing.

For more perspective, some function-oriented languages define their simple (**primitive**) data types, including how they are processed, with classes instead of directly in the compiler. (Handling them in the compiler is faster.) This is an extreme clue to the fact that other classes simply define complex (compound) data types and how they are processed. These compound data types can be composed of any other data types (simple and complex). Further, just as simply typed data can be passed to a method, so can complexly typed data; they are all (logical) objects. With an object passed, the applicable calls from the receiving object can go to methods of the passed object; this is the practical usage of polymorphism. So, any of these calls is actually a *blind (variable) reference to any applicable method.* And an ascendant-class object method is acceptable where its ancestor class is specified (*with the exact same signature*). Then, it can be handled as the ancestor class. This ties back into, and explodes the power of, polymorphism. Simply put, it enables inherited *messages.*

Polymorphism is based on a blind (variable) reference to any applicable method.

Applications have long had individual utility programs, but a class network is a system of utility programs. Third-party software and operating systems have long had some individual utility programs executing, mostly out of the mind of developers, but a class network typically has many little interdependent utility programs executing at the same time, and the developers are very aware of them. This view is reinforced by each language's standard class (network) library, which virtually extends the language itself. Looking at each language as a set of building blocks for applications, each developer class network actually extends the language at a higher level (up a level). A complication, though, is that the standard class network also extends the learning curve for the most efficient programming effort, and the developer class network extends the learning curve for the most efficient (and, therefore, best) designing effort. But function-oriented developers become accustomed enough to this to hardly notice it, just as application-oriented developers become accustomed to copying and modifying code all over an application for a single functional change.

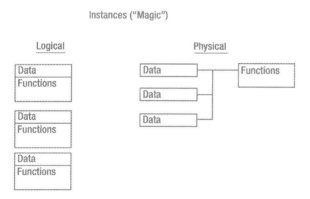

As a cross-check to this entire overview, it's interesting to understand some of what the compiler does "under the hood". It simply translates an object declaration into the corresponding data declarations and links to the lineage's functions (programs), because actually copying the functions would be *extremely* inefficient. Therefore, multiple same-class *logical* objects are *physical* structures (memory-based records), each with a link to the single set of functions; each object creation is an added structure. Each structure is a **namespace**, and the links can be static or dynamic, depending on the function definition. While this understanding removes some of the luster of objects, it makes them clearer, and it does reinforce that this isn't *object* software but object-*oriented* software.

When processes don't require individual dynamic *data* (set at execution time) shared between functions, they don't require explicit objects; these are **class functions**. Looked at from the other direction, the only time an object needs to be created is when a new structure is needed. Also, shared data (static and dynamic) is its own single structure; it's a global object—a **class object**.

All of this also demonstrates that classes are usually best thought of as functions first, then data (items), and objects are best thought of as data (values) first, then functions.

Some Languages

After understanding reasons for its parts, the next aspect that makes learning any language easier is knowing its syntax *structure*, because this makes it much easier to study code samples for syntax details and underlying functionality. The structures of function-oriented languages are particularly tricky. The two most important things to understand are as follows:

- Whereas structure-oriented languages flow smoothly from the beginning to the end of each command (except for parenthesized code, including custom functions in some languages), function-oriented languages have a lot of class interaction (method calls) in many commands. Some of them are *implied*, and many of them might be customized. In essence, a command's flow can be two-dimensional, so tracking execution can be very complex.

- Whereas the most popular structure-oriented languages have plainly labeled commands, the most popular function-oriented languages differentiate many types of commands just by their structure.

GENERATIONS OF LANGUAGES

There is a term, **fourth generation**, regarding programming tools and languages. This term indicates various extents of *pre*compiling—generating code through various types of directives—for specific processing flows. Fourth generation tools serve fairly simple establishing of relationships between the application's components. And fourth-generation languages allow more complex processing, to extend the standard flow, plugged in at points that the fourth-generation system provides. These languages are typically very close to the language of the code generated, varied to facilitate the standard flow.

But nearly never are the previous generations mentioned.

The first generation is machine code. This is often referred to as "1s and 0s", because the most basic computer operation looks at the presence or absence of an electron; presence is represented as 1. The computer strings these together to evaluate combinations of 1s and 0s. The most direct definition of this is binary arithmetic, but the resulting numbers can be thought of in any base. Some of these numbers direct (instruct) the computer what to do with the other numbers, and *those* combinations are the computer operations. The most basic entity is a *binary digit* (bit); the most basic combination is of 8 bits—a *binary term* (byte). Very often, bit values are seen as hexadecimal, because that's reasonably

(continued)

close to decimal, and it uses exactly half of a byte: 16 is 2^4. (And the fact that this operates on electrons is why it's *electronics*.)

The second generation is a fairly direct alphabetic representation of the numbered operations, as words and abbreviations—a *language*, mostly verbs. This is easier for programmers to interpret. It also has the operands of any operation in separate columns, for readability. This configuration must be translated into machine code; a very functional benefit of this step is that the translator can bring together separate pieces of code. So, the second generation entails *assembly*, and its code is an *assembler* language.

The third generation is the one that has been the most common. It's of the languages that are created to serve programmers' points of view. These are also commonly called **high-level languages**, and they include the popular function-oriented languages. In the process of compiling a program, many compilers also interpret directives that affect that whole compilation; these are commonly called **compiler directives**.

The two most popular function-oriented languages are Java and C++, and they have the same syntax structure, although they have a few differing syntax details. This section describes that structure.

The first thing to note with these languages is that methods are identified by the fact that they end with parentheses and, sometimes, a parameter list: `method-name()` or `method-name(parameter-list)` (more specifically, `method-name(data-name,other-data-name)`). Data items—simple and complex—are identified, when they are in the same place as a method could be, by the fact that they *don't* end with parentheses: `data-name`. Arrays use brackets to differentiate their syntax from methods: `data-name[index]`. Also, each array position is indexed minus one: the first item is at `data-name[0]`. Parentheses (and brackets) can be separated from the name by a space.

The next thing to note is that class (and object) members are accessed using a period: `class-name.data-name` or `class-name.method-name()`. (C++ uses other symbols, `::` and `->`, in some situations.) And it's important to keep in mind that case matters: `item` and `Item` are two different items. Further, by convention, class names have their first letter uppercase, and object names—and functions—have their first letter lowercase. Also, by convention, because these names cannot have embedded spaces, multiple word names, of any type, have each word after the first word title-cased (where only the first letter of each word is uppercase): `multipleWordFunction()`.

Braces, { and }, define the beginning and end of a block (of subordinate code), respectively. These are used most frequently in conditionals, method definitions, and class definitions, which are *statements*. And a block can have subordinate blocks. By convention, for some visual clarity, each of the braces is aligned under the beginning of the statement it corresponds to, and the code in the block is indented by four spaces. A variation on the convention puts the left brace at the end of the corresponding statement.

```
statement
{
    subordinate code
}
```

and

```
statement {
    subordinate code
}
```

The simplest command declares usage of a data item. It is of the form

```
data-type data-name
```

and

```
class-name object-name
```

```
data-type [] data-name
```

declares an array.

Common data type names and descriptions are in Table 1-3.

Table 1-3. *Common Data Types*

Category	Data Type	Bytes / Bits	Value Range	COBOL Equivalent
Boolean (true or false)	boolean	– / 1	0 to 1 (false to true, no to yes, off to on)	Nonstandard
Unicode character	char	2 / 16	0 to 65,535 (any character in a Unicode set) [1]	XX
Signed integer	byte	1 / 8	–128 to 127	S99 COMP [–99 to 99]
	short	2 / 16	–32,768 to 32,767	S9(4) COMP [–9,999 to 9,999]
	int	4 / 32	Below –2 billion to above 2 billion	S9(9) COMP [±(1 billion – 1)]
	long	8 / 64	Below –9 quintillion (18 zeroes) to above 9 quintillion	S9(18) COMP [±(1 quintillion – 1)]
Floating-decimal number	float	4 / 32	approx. ±1.4e-045f to ±3.4e+038f (In Java, the f indicates a float.)	Nonstandard
	double	8 / 64	Approx. ±4.9e-324 to ±1.8e+308 [2] (In Java, double is the default floating number.)	Nonstandard

1. *As opposed to ASCII (or EBSIDIC), which is 1 byte per character, Unicode is double byte–based, to accommodate both phonetic characters, as for English, and whole-word characters, as for Chinese.*

2. *The decimal e notation indicates an exponent of 10. For example, 4.9e-324 is 4.9×10^{-324}, which is the decimal followed by 323 zeros, then 49, and is a positive number. 1.8e+308 is 18 followed by 307 zeros, then the decimal.*

This type of command can be prefixed with one or more independent usage indicators:

```
usage usage usage data-type data-name
```

The most common type of usage indicator indicates the usability of the item. The most common usages of this type are **public**, which means that it can be used by any other class; **private**, which means that it *cannot* be used by any other class; and **protected**, which means that it can be used only by ascendant classes. Other types indicate the durability of the item and the rigidity of its definition.

Assignments are of the form

```
data-name = other-data-name
```

and

```
data-name = method-name()
```

and

```
data-name = operation
```

Data item declarations and assignments can be combined. This is common data initialization:

```
data-type data-name = new method-name(parameter-list)
```

Other assignment operators, like +=and *=, simplify self-operation assignments:

```
data-name += other-data-name
```

is equivalent to

```
data-name = data-name + other-data-name
```

Two operators, ++ and --, give +1 and –1 self-assignments a completely different form:

```
data-name++
```

is equivalent to

```
data-name = data-name + 1
```

For comparisons, == is used instead of =, and all comparisons are enclosed in parentheses. It's very clarifying, here, to understand that conditionals most directly test for a true or a false, which means that they test an internal boolean data item. Also, 0 and null translate to false, and everything else translates to true. If an = is ever in a conditional statement, it is doing an assignment first, and the result is tested. Additionally, ! means "not". Several kinds of conditionals are as follows:

if (data-name = -1) is always true.
if (data-name = 0) is always false.
if (data-name == 0) might be true or false.
if (data-name != 0) might be true or false.
if (data-name) tests for the data item being nonzero and non-null.
if (!data-name) tests for the data item being zero or null.
while (true) (and, in C++, while (1), for example) begins an infinite loop, which is broken with a break or a return.

Method declarations closely resemble data declarations, but, instead of the data type defining the method, it's the other way around: the data type is what is returned (to the caller) by the method. Here, the parameter list format is used to *define* the parameter list. Also, void as the data type indicates that the method does not return data to the caller; void as the parameter definition list indicates that the method does not accept data:

usage usage data-type method-name(parameter-definition-list)

more specifically:

data-type method-name(data-type data-name)

and

void method-name(data-type data-name, other-data-type other-data-name)

and

void method-name()

or, in C++

void method-name(void)

Each block has its own **scope** of items. Items declared in a block do not exist outside of that scope. This means that the same exact name in two different scopes represents two different items, including when one scope is a subscope of the other. Also, the this keyword represents the *object* in which it appears.

Deeper into the subject of memory are the **stack** and the **heap**. Basically, the stack holds all of the named items, and the heap holds all of the unnamed items (which are functional because they are pointed to by named items). This is useful because the stack is smaller than the heap, and very large items (objects) on the heap are pointed to by very small items (memory addresses) on the stack. A data declaration creates an item on the stack, and new class-name() creates an object on the heap. class-name is actually a method name that matches the class name; this is a **constructor** method, which initializes the object's data items and returns the address of the object. (This is very important to note because a constructor is invoked any time an object is created.) An object-creation command usually looks redundant, but it is easy to understand what the command is indicating:

```
class-name object-name = new class-name(parameter-list)
```

and

```
ancestor-class-name object-name = new class-name(parameter-list)
```

More specifically, a common example, which looks *very* redundant, is

```
Common common = new Common()
```

It's possible to combine commands through existing parentheses (and brackets):

`method-name(new class-name())` sends the address of the object to the message, and `data-name[index-name++]` looks for the next position in the array.

Another usage of parentheses is in conversion of an item from one type to another, or **casting**. In one way, casting is just helpful, because it saves developers from needing to declare two items, which would need to have different names. Looked at another way, casting is *essential*, because needing to have two items would defeat polymorphism. A cast is declared with parentheses surrounding just a type, *before* the item:

```
data-type data-name = (data-type)other-data-name
```

and

```
data-name = (data-type)method-name(parameter-list)
```

It can be helpful to mentally translate a cast to `<data-type>` to easily differentiate it:

```
data-name = <data-type>method-name(parameter-list)
```

Finally, on the subject of syntax structure, the naming conventions of methods can be misleading in the context of a command. For example, `object.getItem()` does not indicate that that object is getting the item; rather, it indicates that another object is using that object to get the item for itself. It might be helpful to mentally translate this to `object.giveItem()`. Nor does `object.setItem()` indicate that the object is setting the item, but that another object is; it might be helpful to mentally translate it to `object.takeItem()`. These conventions seem to be the opposite of function-oriented thinking. However, `object.isDescription()`, which, by convention, returns a Boolean, is named clearly.

Also, on the subject of just syntax is a point that has not been mentioned until now, so as to not distract from everything else. All commands end with a semicolon, `;`.

An Example of a Class

At this point, a demonstration of how all of the pieces can fit together in a class is appropriate. Here, the language is Java:

```java
public class Rectangle extends Shape {
    private float length;
    private float width;
    public Rectangle (float length, float width) {
        this.length = length;
        this.width = width;
    }
    public float getLength () {
        return length;
    }
    public float getWidth () {
        return width;
    }
    public float perimeter () {
        perimeter (length, width);
        // just in case the class calculation changes
    }
    public static float perimeter (float length, float width) {
        return (2 * (length + width));
    }
    public float area () {
        area (length, width);
        // just in case the class calculation changes
    }
    public static float area (float length, float width) {
        return (length * width);
    }
}
```

Class and function names can be so simple that newcomers may be left wondering what the big deal about them is. Alternately, their usage can involve so many little steps that the newcomers may believe that they're really not worth the extra effort. But their payoff is the ability to swap code—even code by developers who don't even know each other—and that's very common. In practice, then, function orientation has a large factor of industry conformity—of very consistent thinking. (This is a fundamental reinforcement of the fact that function orientation is best served by strong philosophy and consistently accurate vocabulary.) As a bit of strategy, for the best assurance of predictable execution, developers should learn the functionality of each class as it is newly encountered (in others' code), regardless of its source.

Some Differences Between Java and C++

Beyond the syntax structure, C++ is more complex than Java. For example, for some operations, Java uses a descriptive word where C++ uses a symbol. Further, Java doesn't allow some often confusing C++ operations. C++ is committed to supporting C, a language that is very complex because it is more system oriented than developer oriented; C++ pulled C to function orientation. For example, method-name(parameter-list) is an extension of function-name(parameter-list), and class-name.member-name is an extension of structure-name.field-name. A structure is a compound data type without the processes. (A very basic example of C complexity is that, even though the function-name(parameter-list) syntax is based on the mathematical function syntax, it's actually very different. In math, $f(x)$ means that x is the focus, and f serves x; in C, very often f is the focus, and x serves f. This is plainly evidenced in the fact that the parentheses can occur without anything in them. And the syntax is an example of *over*extension of a concept.)

Java, a younger language than C++, was created to be committed to function orientation, then to C++ syntax; Java pulled function orientation to C++. C++ allows extreme control over a system, which also allows the most possible efficiency during program execution, so it is generally thought of as the most powerful language. But, in a different way, Java can be thought of as the most powerful language, because it allows the most possible efficiency during program *development*: Java was designed on how C++ is mostly *used*. This view is supported by all of function orientation. Function orientation causes the computer to do more during execution than it would have to for a structured program, but the development efficiency is worth the execution inefficiency. Further, the increasing speed of computers decreases the impact of inefficiency, and Java is becoming more efficient as it matures (being redesigned on how *Java* is mostly used). Besides, ultimately, computers are supposed to do as much productive work as possible.

An example of C++ complexity—and extreme confusion—is its memory address management, which came from C. Java does this implicitly for objects and doesn't allow it otherwise. The result is that, in Java, pointers are not directly accessible (and references don't require an identifying character). Table 1-4 is the simplest possible explanation of C++'s memory address management, as it appears in code; this table might not be found in any other books. By the way, the *type* of address is important because it indicates the length, then the data type, of the item in the heap.

Table 1-4. *C++ Memory Address Management*

Operator X Context	data-type **Suffix:** Definition / Parameter Declaration	data-type **Suffix:** Initialization (Left of =) / Binding (Parameter)	data-name **Prefix:** Usage / Return Declaration
& (**reference**)	*Is* address of type data-type, with * *usage implied*[1]	*Get* address of right/passed	*Get* address of data-name
* (**pointer**)	*Is* address of type data-type	Get data at address right/passed	Get data at address data-name

1. *For perspective, a data name is an internal (language-level) reference.*

Further, C++ allows pointer manipulation, which can easily lead to reading something that is supposed to be unattainable and writing something in the wrong place, corrupting data—even of unrelated applications. Java doesn't allow pointer manipulation. Similarly, C++ allows an array index to be set to *any* integer, regardless of array size; this then translates to a memory address, and the same corruption can occur. So, the programmer must always manually program a check for array overflow and underflow (where the index is less than zero). Java, very simply, does this automatically.

Another example of C++ complexity also regarding memory is memory reclamation when an object is no longer referenced by other objects. Without proper memory reclamation, a program is more likely to run out of memory. In C++, this must be coded specifically by the programmer, who must mentally track when an object is *likely* no longer referenced by other objects, or the programmer must create a tracking mechanism for each object. (Because of the specific programming, C++ also has a "destructor" method. Its name is the same as the class name, prefixed by a tilde: `~class-name()`.) Java has a built-in tracking mechanism and an automatic memory reclamation process termed **garbage collection**.

In short, Java is smoother than C++. Further, Java is actually more function oriented than C++. For one thing, it defaults any method to support polymorphism, whereas C++ requires an explicit usage (because polymorphism isn't of the highest execution efficiency). For another thing, Java has everything defined in a class, including `main()`. C++ has `main()` defined in a file that might or might not have any class definitions (because C++ is file oriented, because its core is C).

But Java isn't *perfectly* clear, either. Sometimes it tries to be a little bit *too* smooth, and this is actually counterproductive to clarity. The big culprit here is its overuse (overloading) of the **period** (or **dot**) **operator**. Again, Java uses `.` to indicate things like `class-name.data-name` and `object-name.method-name()`, but it also uses `.` to indicate the levels of a package (library) structure and the levels of a class family. Further, it uses `.` to indicate `.class`, which is a mechanism that dynamically analyzes objects. Still further, it uses `.` to indicate a "chaining" of command parts, which syntactically merges the output of a method with a member name. All of these uses make this logical syntax possible:

```
pkg-lvl1.pkg-lvl2.base-class.derived-class.object.class.method().data
```

Using four *differing* operators for clarity, this could be mentally translated to

```
/pkg-lvl1/pkg-lvl2\base-class\derived-class.object.class.method():data
```

Though it's a little misleading, the fact that `.class` is a constant makes it fairly clear.

Along with all of that, the period operator makes the two-dimensional processing (interobject method calls) very inconspicuous, especially when an object name is the same as a convention word or a keyword from another language—for example, "is" (abbreviating, for example, `InputStream`) or "from". It must be remembered that, regardless of the appearance of the words, execution always jumps to that object, which then executes that method, and *then* the rest of the command gets executed.

Some Hardware and Software Manufacturers

There are many manufacturers of hardware and many more manufacturers of software (operating systems or applications). A few companies manufacture both hardware and software. The following are some of the most relevant hardware and software manufacturers.

Apple Computer

Apple Computer and its Macintosh computer are often at the leading edge of user interfaces and hardware, in both designs and features. For the Macintosh, Apple created the first operating system based on a graphical user interface (GUI), using a *pointing device* (mouse), *pictures* (icons), and *windows*. The Mac OS now also includes the Sherlock computer search and Safari network-integrated search-and-presentation programs.

Just a few of Apple's hardware innovations, since its founding in the 1970s, are the assembled microcomputer (personal computer), dynamically identified plug-in devices (hot swapping), the personal data assistant (PDA), the docked portable PC (the PowerBook), the flat-screen monitor and the mouse pad (both for the PowerBook), the optical mouse, the one-unit PC (the iMac), the portable MP3 player (the iPod), and the dial pad (for the iPod).

Apple is the largest manufacturer of both hardware and software for personal computers, and it now creates the most computer units built on a version of the UNIX operating system (platform).

NeXT Inc., started by Apple cofounder Steve Jobs, was in many ways at the leading edge in software development environments. It is now owned by Apple, and its development environment is now the basis for Apple's.

Sun Microsystems

Sun Microsystems is the creator of the Java language and much of Java's supporting development software. The Java environment is, in other ways, at the leading edge of software development.

Sun also manufactures computers built on a version of UNIX, although with a different set of GUIs from Apple's. In varying ways, both Apple and Sun gear their products to be multiplatform compatible.

Other Originators

The GUI approach was created by Xerox Corporation.

AT&T was the originator of both UNIX and C++.

Netscape widely popularized the network (web) browser.

Microsoft

Microsoft thoroughly develops its versions of the software of these and other companies, specifically dedicated to its operating systems.

Some Other Languages

Besides Java and C++, a few other function-oriented languages are widely used.

C#

A newer language from Microsoft is C# (pronounced "C sharp"). Despite its name, it's most succinctly described as Java with some C++ features used in controlled ways. It also incorporates some Java *conventions* into the compiler. For example, in Java, properties (private data items) are identified by the access function naming convention of the property name preceded by "get" (for reading) or "set" (for writing). In C#, there's an actual property item that can have get and set clauses as part of its definition; instead of function calls, these are invoked with (public) data item reference syntax (`object.data` and even `object.data = value` for the writing). This device is creative, and enforcing controlled property access is important, but the implied processing (from misdirecting syntax) can be confusing.

Objective C and Smalltalk

For some perspective here, two other popular function-oriented languages, which have a very different (segmented) syntax structure, are Smalltalk and Objective C. Smalltalk was created by Xerox and is generally thought of as the purest function-oriented language. Objective C was developed by NeXT, is Smalltalk syntax built on top of C syntax, and is Apple's language of choice. In effect, Objective C makes a clear visual distinction between its function-oriented and non-function-oriented parts. Smalltalk's and, therefore, Objective C's syntax is less flowing, which makes it at first a little awkward, but it is *visually* more function oriented, so its functionality is clearer. Java, in bringing function orientation to C++, is actually based on Smalltalk's underlying functionality, which makes Objective C very easy for Java veterans to understand, on many levels. Its syntax is described very briefly in this section.

A colon is used with a *label* (by convention) to indicate each method parameter and is included in the method name (along with the root part of the message name) when the method has parameters. In a message, the parameters are split with a space. For example, there's `class-name root`, as in `Rectangle area`, and `object-name rootLabel1:Label2:`, as in `aRectangle setWidth:Height:`, which is called with `object-name rootLabel1:data-name1 Label2:data-name2`, as in `aRectangle setWidth:x Height:y`. So, each method's purpose is more obvious, which makes it much simpler to learn how to use all of the functions of a class network. (By the way, it means that there is no actual overloading.)

Objective C encloses the message in brackets—for example, `[Rectangle area]`—which easily visually differentiates (Smalltalk-type) nonparameter messages from (C-type) data declarations, which otherwise look identical, so the brackets must be paid attention to here. The brackets also support very clear chaining. A common message, equivalent to Java/C++'s `new class-name()`, is `[[class-name alloc] init]`.

On another topic, Smalltalk has only dynamic data types (automatic casting), to support polymorphism; its data declarations don't include a data type. One of the main reasons that Objective C was created was to effectively add static data typing to Smalltalk, because all dynamic data typing is inefficient. In fact, Objective C method declarations look like Smalltalk with C casting for the root (for the return) and each parameter: `(data-type)rootlabel1:(data-type1)data-name1`. So, in Objective C (as opposed to Java/C++), method declarations look very distinct from data declarations.

Objective C has pointers (because C does), but it treats them the *same* as references, with brackets, so Objective C's memory address management is much simpler than C++'s. Also, Objective C has a built-in object tracking mechanism (`retain` and `release`), so its memory reclamation is much simpler than C++'s and more effective than Java's.

Visual Basic

Another highly popular function-oriented language is Visual Basic, which was developed by Microsoft. Visual Basic has a more plain-language basis than the rest, even title-casing its keywords. It has less punctuation, and so is wordier, which also makes it relatively easy to learn—it's like the COBOL of function-oriented languages. It also follows the functionality of Java much more than of C++; it actually now has exactly the same functionality as C#.

Even all the way down to data item declaration, Visual Basic's syntax is different (while the effect is the same): `Dim data-name As data-type`. It doesn't have simplified self-assignment operators (like `+=` and `++`), but its comparison syntax is simpler (without the required outer parentheses and `==`), like COBOL. However, it requires any `Not` to immediately follow the `If`, instead of allowing it to immediately precede the operator. This tends to make the `Not` too inconspicuous, but a trailing inline comment can help there:

```
If Not data-item = other-data-item Then    ' <Not
```

Also in Visual Basic, blocks are implicit, so they don't require the braces, but they do require one of various `End` commands. And Visual Basic's commands aren't terminated with a colon; instead, its much less frequent multiline commands are continued with an underscore, `_`.

Visual Basic mostly doesn't use parentheses with its methods; these are necessary only within a specific type of assignment, when a data item is receiving the value of the return item of a method that is called with parameters. This makes the appearance of the vast majority of method references very friendly (for example, `Selection.Find.Replacement.Text`). But any of the nodes can be either an object reference or a method reference, so, unlike the other popular languages, this identification isn't immediately obvious and requires an investigation effort.

Incremental Adaptation

Looking at the relationship between application-oriented and function-oriented designs, the most straightforward way to transition a software system from application-oriented to function-oriented is to gather related functions into a set, set by set. A secondary effort is probably needed, as one second pass over the entire system or multiple passes over functional sections, to optimize the interaction among the sets (classes). The second pass effort is actually part of some popular function-oriented software development processes. Really, the application might not need to be made *entirely* function oriented; maybe only the sets that change frequently, or haven't changed only because of a foreseen complex effort, need to be reoriented.

•

■ ■ ■

CHAPTER TWO

Bi-design
Function-Oriented Designing Strategies

This chapter describes a comprehensive set of simple function-oriented designing philosophies and a dynamic overall strategy for applying them in various situations.

Analyzing

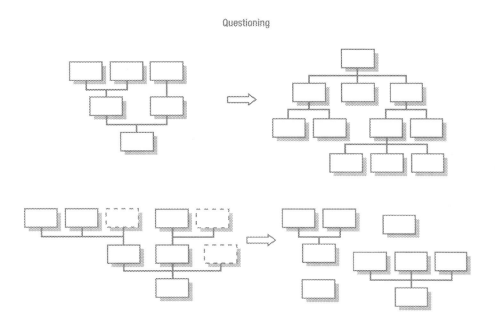

Questioning

It's fairly unknown that analyzing for even application orientation is best served by a parallel process of structured questioning. This always requires starting by asking, "What is the purpose of the application?" Then, the questions regarding all of the major objectives are asked; then, the questions for all of the next level; and so on. The direct result of the questioning is a full analysis, from the highest to the lowest levels. (It's interesting to notice, here, that a family of questions builds a hierarchy of analysis.) And it's best to inform the involved users of the question structure ahead of any involved meetings, so that they will best be prepared to provide the answers.

Because of the bidirectional balance, analyzing for function orientation requires a new area of analyzing questioning: "What is the purpose of the *design*?" "Reasonably, how will it change, and how will it be used for other applications, later?" This additional area can be appropriate at any point in the questioning. And the more broadly flexible the software must be—for example, for specific-application-building *frameworks* and, especially, for generic *toolkits*—the more complex the interaction mechanisms must be. (It should be noted that a toolkit is very often *called* a framework. Actually, either can encompass the other. A large framework can use multiple toolkits, and a single tool can use a small framework; in fact, a single class can qualify as either.) This is a more complex process of questioning, which results in a more complex analysis. It is bidirectional questioning, for a bidirectional analysis; it can also be seen as more *complete* questioning for more *complete* analysis.

In the absence of the ability to conduct thorough questioning, and even in addition to it, to clarify or verify some of the answers, the ability to analyze code has always been essential for the most complete designs. A designer should be able to look at code and feel what it is doing, instantly translating it to functionality. It is, therefore, important to understand the thinking of languages and their features—to have a feel for, and then to know in detail, what the language is doing behind the code. Further, a strong strategy for streamlined development has designing partially built around—*derived from*—coding. This is based on a set of organized processes of optimization known as **refactoring**. It provides confidence in changes, because it integrates automated unit testing and specifically points out the potential problems to pay attention to with each type of change. It doesn't have exact rules on *when* to make each type of change, because each requires the context of the system—what it is and what it needs to be. In support of function orientation's advantage of centralized changes, it actually creates a further level of flexibility; with it, the network itself is not overcommitted. Together, they allow the continually simplest design that provides the total identified functionality. Ultimately, they allow designing on demand.

Tracking Execution

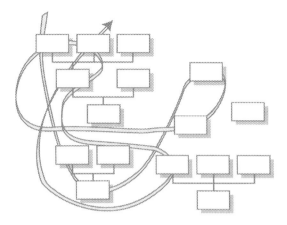

Regardless of those important skills, analysis gets a huge head-start from being able to see an application run—especially, to *monitor* its running with diagnostic tools. And whatever aspects are working well can usually be treated one-dimensionally; in other words, its code doesn't need to be analyzed. Very often, a system objective is code that executes as quickly as possible. The deepest idiosyncrasies of languages often become the focus of this objective (and this focus is best accomplished by programmers). But, ultimately, these factors have less impact on speed than the many factors of the underlying logic—the many levels of the system design. And, at its deepest levels, function-oriented designing is very simple. But, in total, the need to jump from set to set to follow interdependent processing can become very complex; this is the source of particular danger in a function set network, so it must be managed well.

Ultimately, the deepest idiosyncrasies of languages have less impact on speed than the many factors of the system design.

The philosophy of simplicity extends to the selection of third-party utilities (toolkits and frameworks). They are integral to function-oriented software, because its inherent swapability makes toolkits and frameworks easier to both use and change at will (than with application-oriented software), so they are abundant parts of these systems. This is possible with standardized interfaces and standardized functionality. But it's crucial to hold as a guide that any utilities are better when they are less invasive to the software that is using them. This means that they shouldn't force significant changes—functional contortions— to that software; they should strive to allow transparency. So, the philosophy of simplicity extends to the standards as well. It also points out that *any* designing must take into account that control can be shifted, to varying degrees, to the *using* function sets or the *used* function sets; this is in consideration of the users' (developers') balance between the ability to *choose* low-level functions and the ability to *focus* on high-level functionality.

Most of a system's documentation is best accomplished within the code. And most of *that* is best accomplished through practices of clear naming, limited function scoping and, as a cross-check, automated testing. This maximizes dynamic documentation, which absolutely minimizes the need to coordinate documentation with code changes—and strongly facilitates refactoring and designing on demand. In essence, the best way to document and test a system is to let the compiler in on as much of the design as possible. Most function-oriented languages support the process of **reflection**, which is a *live* summary documentation, for the system itself; this can easily be used to generate dynamic summary documentation.

Coding practices, testing modules, and nonobvious comments minimize the need to coordinate documentation with code. The best way to document and test a system is to let the compiler in on as much of the design as possible.

The clearest picture of an unfamiliar class comes from a complete listing of its functions, which is most effective as soon as the class is encountered. In (static) reference documentation, it's common to see functions listed in alphabetical order; this easily becomes a fairly nonfunctional pile of information. The most functional listing is in order of common usage, then in order of common chronology. This is best accomplished, with dynamic documentation, by ordering the actual groups of functions in this way. At the family level, this ordering can be accomplished with a hand-sorted class table. Separate documentation is best for the most basic things—for example, where to find all of the code. This approach is actually an example of loose coupling.

Designing

Inside of a Set

Fragmented

Grouped

A
B
1
2
a
b

A
1
a
B
2
b

The heart of function orientation might be most simply identified by a parallel. A group of functions can have many levels of logic. Each level can be a function of its own, which is located directly after the next higher level (its calling function) or sequentially after others of the same level. So, two functions of the same level can be separated by lower-level functions. Drawn out, the effect is of each level *wrapping* the ones below it. The tangible benefit of this is that any functional group is one contiguous segment of code, and moving any functional group is one big step—instead of many little steps. This is an extension to function-oriented concepts. (An even simpler parallel and extension is the organization of a multidimensional array. Grouping items of the same owner together, instead of items of the same type, allows all of the items of any owner to be copied in one big step, instead of many little steps.)

But, again, function orientation is more complex than these parallels because it has interacting *types* of function sets and, therefore, interaction mechanisms—which, again, can have characteristics of being alive.

Mechanism Characteristics

After learning the ingredients of, and appropriate situations for, each type of mechanism, the most effective objective for designers is to develop both a feeling for the capabilities and limitations of the entire set of mechanism types *and* a feeling for how to orchestrate combinations of their usage, in one task and across a system. To achieve these feelings, one must understand the *meaning* of each mechanism type and think through applications based on functionality. To comprehensively serve that, this section describes the more-basic meaning of each of several language features.

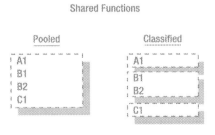

A very simple example of the meaning of a language feature regards *class* data and *class* functions. These are constants, variables shared among instances, and functions performed on only external variables—shared variables, parameters, and other objects' data items. Except where the shared variables are concerned, these items are available to any object of a differing class without instantiating the first class. There are a couple of meanings here. The more straightforward one is that some data and functions are exactly the same in every object of that class. But the more significant one is that these items are not just kept in one big pool; they are kept in logical groupings, each with the appropriate function set, which serves change and adaptation efforts. (Also, the class language feature reinforces that the software is fundamentally more function oriented than object oriented.)

Items are not just kept in one big pool; they are kept in logical groupings, each with the appropriate function set, which serves change and adaptation efforts.

Another very simple example regards *abstract* functions. These are most often described as functions that have no implementation, existing only to establish their interface; one ascendant class in each lineage has the responsibility of establishing the implementation for that interface (and others have the option). But another type of abstract function has just enough implementation to establish how it uses other functions; this is commonly known as a **Template** mechanism type. (This is very appropriate for a framework.) In either case, an abstract function is meant to serve polymorphism, which requires a common interface. A *class* is abstract when it has at least one abstract function. (Java has a class type explicitly defined as an interface, which has *all* abstract functions. It is "implemented" [instead of extended] to a concrete class.)

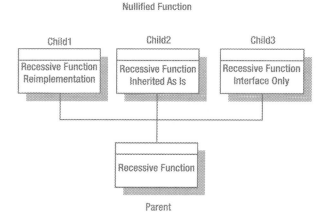

Another simple, but often frowned on, example regards the fact that ascendant functions can *nullify* ancestor functions (when they are virtual). Virtual functions are dynamically loaded, at execution, so they are meant to be dynamically replaced with overriding functions, but any can actually be overridden with a null function. This is discouraged because each child is supposed to either propagate or build on its parent's characteristics, but that can sometimes make extending a family complicated; and that's really not necessary, because a virtual function can be interpreted, in the vocabulary of a family, as a "recessive gene" (which might, in any generation, go away). Of course, this should probably be an exception, especially for considerations of memory usage.

Core function-oriented concepts can be clearly understood in terms of more-everyday parallels.

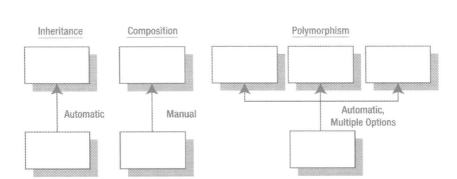

Making Connections

- **Binding** (or, in older terminology, **linkage**) can be thought of as a connection, as follows. Inheritance is an **implicit connection**; it is automatically part of a class. Composition is an **explicit connection**; it requires specific code. And polymorphism is a **dynamic connection**; it is determined by execution conditions.

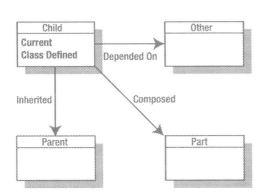

Sources of Functionality

- Methods can be thought of in the following ways. Inherited methods are **inherent functions**, composed methods are **adopted functions**, and current-class-defined methods are **created functions**. Regarding another property of living entities, associated (external) methods are **interdependent functions**.

Characteristics

Genetics + Enviroment + x = 1

- Attributes can be seen as defining the uniqueness (the unique combination of characteristics) of a class, attributed to a combination of influences. Inherited attributes are **genetic characteristics**, composed attributes are **environmental characteristics**, and current-class-defined attributes are **differential characteristics**. (By the way, the concept of a differential characteristic addresses the fact that living entities do not *perfectly* copy their genetic or environmental characteristics.)

The same core concepts can be looked at from a different direction, in terms of how each is implemented in code. Inheritance is accomplished in a **class declaration**, with a clause. Composition has two forms: static composition is specified with **data declarations**, which show that the class manages objects of other classes, for a particular set of purposes; and dynamic composition (polymorphism) is specified with **data declarations using function parameters,** which show that the object manages other objects. **Aggregation** (organized object collection) is defined with a **dynamic composition hierarchy**, which establishes grouped object references. And dependence is demonstrated by using **messages**, within one class or through a combination of classes; this is indirect usage. Table 2-1 summarizes these implementations.

Table 2-1. *Core Concepts in Code*

Concept	Implementation
Inheritance	Class declaration
Composition, static	Data declaration
Composition, dynamic	Data declaration using parameter passed in
Aggregation	Set of data declaration using parameters passed in
Dependence	Message

There are arguments both for and against a class having more than one parent (plus the parent that is the step of the designing process), the condition known as **multiple inheritance**. There are times when a class could logically inherit from two (or more) different classes, each accounting for a different aspect of the inheriting class. (For example, a square is both a rectangle and a rhombus.) But the compilation of a multiple inheritance in which each parent class has the same-named function causes a conflict, which must be resolved with explicit (manual) decision making for each conflict. (For example, a rectangle's area involves its length and its width, while a rhombus's involves its length and its acute angle; further, a square's involves just its length.) In essence, for each, it must be determined which parent has the dominant gene and which have the recessive; generally, the dominant function is the one that has the most functionality. This is resolved in a wholesale way— sometimes by convention, sometimes by language restriction—by combining only one class for implementations with any number of classes for interfaces.

In any case, it must be remembered that multiple inheritance is a *logical* condition; common functions must be manually overridden to accommodate the combination. Simplifying that work, generically, the copied implementation of a recessive function can remain, intact, *inside* of the copied dominant one, maybe just tailored to it. The simplest situation allows the recessive parent function to just be called from the copied dominant function.

In a related matter, all phases of the development process are greatly facilitated by a particular level of documentation: just as application orientation always begged descriptions of programs—files, records, and data items; and procedure sections, groupings, and complex statements—function orientation also begs descriptions of interaction mechanisms. Often, a mechanism requires a setup, and sometimes it also requires a reset; these should be clearly documented as well.

Function orientation begs descriptions of interaction mechanisms.

RELATING TO INTERACTION ALGEBRA

As mentioned in the Introduction and covered in Chapter Four, **interaction algebra** is a notation that enables a very structured, very concise technique for analyzing interactions and designing mechanisms.

Perhaps the most far-reaching ability of interaction algebra is how it might be able to thoroughly clarify *combinations* of mechanisms as an integral part of a whole-system design. Just as in standard algebra, the objective is to maintain the algebraic characteristics—manipulating variables, not inserting constants. Of course, in both, this type of effort can be cumbersome, but (in both) it's often necessary.

At a slightly lower level, there's the topic of programming languages; a language can be seen as simply a *tool* of designing. The effects particular languages have on the design are obviously important to consider, especially in choosing which language to use. The most significant issue related to function orientation is binding. C++ has mostly static binding. The pro to this is that C++ does most of its memory-map construction at compile time, so it is faster at execution. The cons are that it requires heavy recompiling, it does not have (execution-time) object analysis features, and it is not extensible by the user. Java and Objective C have mostly dynamic binding, and Smalltalk has *only* dynamic binding. The con is that they do most of their memory-map construction at execution time, so they are slower. The pros are that they do not require heavy recompiling, they do have object analysis features, and they are extensible by the user (including by other systems—*the ultimate in software reuse*).

Network Characteristics

At a much *higher* level, it can be seen that a network of function sets actually has an *embedded* structure, which includes levels, but not an overall hierarchy. While an application-oriented view of a system is a breakdown of its objectives, which is an *obvious* structure, a function-oriented view of the same system is a breakdown of its functionality—a structure of *types* of function sets. These types are defined by each set's role in an interaction mechanism and, moreover, by its role in potential applications. The more meaningful roles are architectural **aspects** (or **concerns**). *A network can be seen to be most simply a **virtual hierarchy**, meaning that it's basically a hierarchy with loose connections, providing options.*

A network of function sets actually has an embedded structure—a breakdown of its types of function sets. A network can be seen to be most simply a virtual hierarchy, with loose connections.

Dependence is a network in its simplest form, because it has no structure. In the next simplest (and more common) form, a function set network has *static* composition hierarchies. Beginning to be complex, this network can be functionally extended with dynamic composition. More complex, the differing types of function sets can be brought together only through application classes (or groups of classes) and their static composition. (This type of connection is a **Mediator** mechanism type, and a system that uses only these can be said to have a Mediator architecture [or a segmented-Mediator architecture].) And most complex, the application classes can have dynamic composition. Any network can have combinations of all of these. The reason why the more complex connections are often better is that they make the network structure more flexible. Actually, a network connected entirely through dependence is much worse than an application-oriented system, because it has much more complexity (of logic spread over many modules and a lot of jumping around at execution) but no more benefit. And a network connected entirely through application classes with only dynamic composition is, on its own, usually too complex for any of its benefits. A significant exception is when this is handled through a third-party framework that uses a parameter description file as the dynamic composition; an example of this type of framework is Spring.

The connections between function sets can make a network structure anywhere from very rigid to very flexible, even in various places at the same time.

Function orientation reorients structure; it anchors structure at the level of the function set, instead of at the level of the entire system. System-level structure is too flexible for ongoing design; it allows little patches (ultimately promoting laziness) that *violate higher objectives and, therefore, corrupt the structure.* This same violation is evident, on a different scale, when programmers devise extremely creative C code to ease the programming task. The severe problem with this freedom is that it unnecessarily complicates code changes, especially by other programmers, but even for the original programmer, none of whom will really understand how the extremely creative code actually does what it does! The concept of function sets—each with a cohesive purpose—is a reinforcing consideration that guides the ongoing design; *it explicitly identifies when the higher objectives have changed.* This means that, ideally, function-oriented systems shouldn't need massive overhauls; they get periodic limited overhauls.

Anchoring structure at the level of the function set, instead of at the level of the entire system, function orientation guides the ongoing design; *it explicitly identifies when the higher objectives have changed.*

In function-oriented designing, it is fairly common practical advice that, while inheritance (and, especially, polymorphism) is a very interesting feature of function orientation, composition should be used much more frequently. This is because specializing multiple classes adds up to multiple children; further specialization adds multiple children of the previous ones. This makes a class network unnecessarily complex; multiplication is much better managed by *combining* one new class with the old ones. Simply put, inheritance should be used only when a function must have changes *inserted* or when an object must be *implicitly* replaced. But it is extremely uncommon to hear that there is very strong philosophy behind that advice. Inheritance is another way of saying *static adaptation*; likewise, polymorphism is another way of saying *dynamic adaptation*. These are not to be confused with *adaptability*, which is the greatest benefit of function orientation. At each step, then, the comparison is composition versus adaptation. Basically, in constructing an application, each instance of adaptation depletes adaptability.

Inheritance and polymorphism are adaptations. In constructing an application, each instance of adaptation depletes adaptability. Inheritance should be used only when a function must have changes *inserted* or when an object must be *implicitly* replaced. Multiplication is much better managed by combining one new class with the old ones.

Applying Philosophy

Philosophy must be practically applicable to be of any real value. The pure philosophy behind the origin of function-oriented software was a desire to *study*—and, therefore, model—real-world system behaviors, *with an unknown end result.* Real-world behaviors include adaptability, which turns out to be a great benefit for everyday business software.

But business units seldom need to *study* real-world behaviors; they *know* their *own* basic behaviors. They simply need to model their behaviors in their software for it to best *serve* those behaviors—and future behaviors that can be derived from them. Developing models for study incurs more overhead than business units generally need, so *the original function orientation philosophy is not fully applicable.*

Pure function-oriented software is designed to *study* behaviors, with an *unknown* end result. Business function-oriented software is designed to *serve known* behaviors.

A philosophical balance is needed in function-oriented designing, to accommodate any of multiple purposes. This section delineates a dynamic overall strategy, which is a product of idealism meeting reality—of developmental purity meeting budgetary efficiency. It has built-in flexibility, which explicitly addresses the competing needs of various development situations. Actually, this explicit strategy is a balance commonly utilized in business software development, but it's just not much mentioned (or maybe even explicitly noticed—speaking of studying real-world behaviors). And, of course, *any* strategy at least implicitly requires continual tuning of the design, through partial redesigning. The main objective of this strategy is the same process for any situation: to identify basically all of the function sets (the overall whats) of the system.

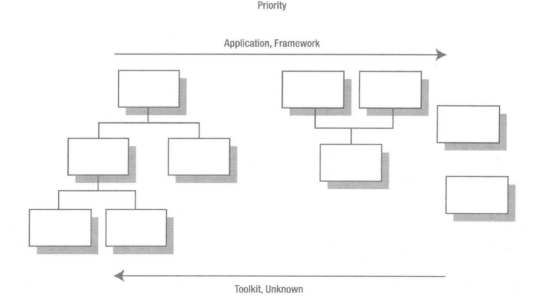

To clarify the rest of the strategy, in support of the main objective, the bidirectional nature of the function-oriented designing process must be approached from one direction, secondarily accommodating the other. The choice is based on the highest priority of the design—*its* purpose. Approaching the identification from the *structure* direction, secondarily accommodating the network, is more appropriate for a single application or a framework, which is ultimately an application that has design variables built in to it. Approaching the process from the *network* direction, secondarily accommodating structures, is more appropriate for a toolkit or an unknown end result, which is the characteristic of open-ended research. Really, though, the situations that are appropriate for directly approaching from the network direction are best served by an accumulation of understanding of function interactions from the structure direction, through previous indirect efforts. So, to put it most simply, a typical function set network is generated partly through the process of "*de*composition".

A typical function set network is generated partly through the process of "*de*composition".

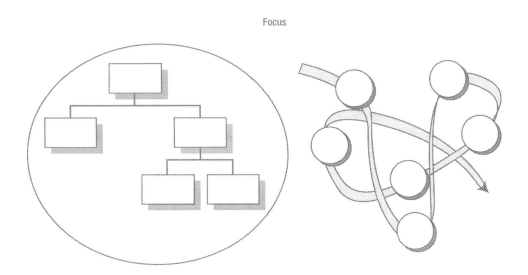

Focus

Ultimately, anchoring in structure is very objective, which makes it a very solid guide. It is driven by analysis of **functional significance**, which requires the whole system to be kept in mind, continually. From the structure direction, once the function sets are identified, each system objective is broken down, and the component functions fall into the appropriate set. Anchoring in nonstructure is very subjective, which makes it a very risky guide, with a wider range of possible outcomes. It is driven by analysis of **sequential execution**, which keeps focus on system *segments*. Done well, a nonstructure is more flexible in building multiple structures; done poorly, a nonstructure makes building *any* structure extremely tedious.

Another Layer

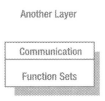

The fact that the whole-system collection of function sets *is* a network requires a layer of design more than that for a structure. This layer addresses the whole design of the *communication among the function sets*—the means to manage them. Hierarchically, then, this layer is at the top of the design—above the function sets themselves. But it is definitely *part* of the design—part of the system *functions*. More practically, the aspect of the design it pertains to is the whole set of interfaces. And the choice of direction— structure or network—affects the complexity of the set of interfaces; the network (multi-application) approach frequently requires more sophisticated interaction mechanisms than does the structure (uniapplication) one.

True Orientation

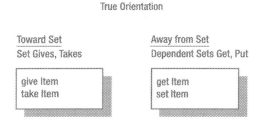

Throughout the designing process, regardless of the approach, it is necessary to balance consideration of collections of entities with consideration of each individual entity. Here, the most important thing to keep in mind is that a design—particularly a function-oriented design—is geared to the *future*. Violating the integrity of a function set, to make the current design process easier, borrows on the future. This philosophy is well served by the true object-oriented mind-set that sees data item manipulation functions as "give" and "take" (as opposed to the common "get" and "set").

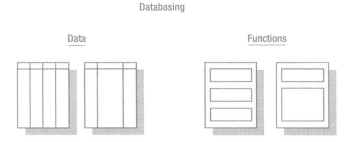

As the designing of an actual system unfolds, just as classes can be seen to simply define complex (compound) data types and how they are processed, class designing can be seen to basically be the *databasing of functions*. There are many similarities between class designing and standard database designing; there's a common feel, especially for relational databases (the most common modern databases), because they dynamically link tables (logical files), with one having the parameters for another. (This view is reinforced by the capability of embedded SQL, with which tables also store the code for common functions.) Basically, in both types of designing, the combinations of similarities and differences define how entities can be shared. But, again, function orientation has added complexity. Function databasing can be seen as an inheritance of standard databasing, with more factors to balance. Sharing needs determine whether all of the functions of a set should go into one class or a group (a team) of classes—function subsets. And, as in any type of designing, there are always balances of consideration of space versus time; an extension of this, for function orientation, is the consideration of static versus dynamic entities.

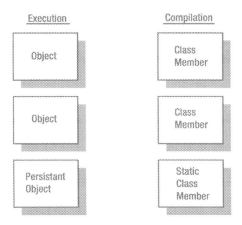

Further, whether a function requires (execution-time) state determines whether the design requires an object, or a group of objects, beyond a class. From a very function-oriented point of view, it can be seen that classes are actually compile-time states of a family; more basically, it can be seen that an implementation is a compile-time instantiation of an interface. The analyzing process tends to lend itself to identifying these states first as singular objects. Then, observing the constants that are present, the further properties of classes tend to become identified. Finally, assessing similarities and differences between class usages tends to be required to identify class groups (to optimize the family); it also is very helpful in identifying how the classes should be instantiated, with the "creational" category of interaction mechanisms.

At this point, it's interesting to examine concepts of an *object-oriented database*. First of all, storing objects actually means just storing the data items of those objects, not the functions; it's about persistent execution-time *state*. Further, it must be remembered that it's not about storing classes; it's about storing *lineages*. The accurate representation of objects in a relational database is of one row (in one table) containing an instance of a lineage—objects of multiple classes. The whole reason for the idea of an object-oriented database is the fact that relational databases have limited compatibility with objects. For example, as a fundamental relational rule, no table is allowed to contain (encapsulate) arrays, and table references to other tables are by column (data item) value, whereas object references to other objects are by object (memory) location. These complications are most easily managed with object-to-table mapping—commonly called **object-relational (OR) mapping**—encapsulated in objects that connect the original objects to the database; this technique is a very common way to implement an object-*oriented* database. A packaged object-oriented database can most simply house (encapsulate) the mapping objects, effectively presenting internal tables as objects.

An *object* database, actually storing objects *as* objects, at the very least requires changing each object reference to an internally schemed (database) location. A relational database is very good for dynamic (selective) retrieval because its tables have indexes on key columns; objects don't have indexes, but an object *database* can. Also, because related lineages share some ancestry, families are appropriately represented with tabular metadata, indicating, for example, the boundaries of consecutive columns corresponding to each class. (Metadata *defines* data.) It's very grounding to examine a class database at the highest level, in light of all of this: the main usage of a class database is a *derivation* of the usage of a *relational* database, because it exists at compile time.

Organization of Context

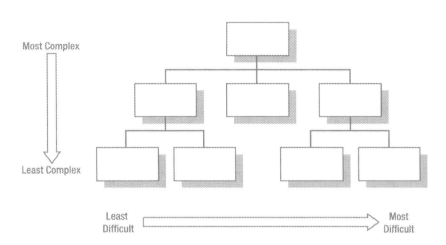

An efficient class network design can be arrived at in various ways. But some *support* how class groups fit together, and some *conflict* with it. Assessing each segment of the system through narrowing context ensures supporting identification; this effort goes hand-in-hand with structure-driven network designing (and decomposition). And structure designing is best served by a particular strategy, which also is the source of some debate. Anchoring this process in organization, the entire structure progresses downward from the most complex to the least complex tasks, which is to say that the levels progress from the most-combined simple tasks to the least-combined; this is the same as structure designing for application-oriented software. (A parallel to this progression can be seen in packing a suitcase, for which, basically, the biggest articles should be packed first, the next smaller things packed around them, and so on.) At each level, the tasks are usually best arranged in the opposite direction, from the least difficult to the most; this is noticeably different from structure designing for application-oriented software, for which each level is chronological. One exception, here, is that an important task *might* be most appropriate in a specific place; this can be considered a framework for other tasks. (In the suitcase parallel, this would be the suitcase itself.) Another exception is that a task that is dependent on another task *must* occur after that other task; so, each level is usually *partially* chronological.

IMPORTANCE

1. INTERFACE

2. IMPLEMENTATION

There are, of course, limits on what are reasonable efforts for any designing, and they depend on the exact priorities of the situation and the situations it is a part of. As some trade-offs are always necessary, it's helpful to keep in mind that, ultimately, interface is more important than implementation. In other words, int*er*-entity efficiency is more important than int*ra*-entity efficiency, simply because the main point of function orientation is that development efficiency is more important than execution efficiency. Also, this is another way of looking at the fact that communication among function sets manages them. As a parallel, from the *user's* point of view, interface is more important than implementation. In other words, excellent system internals can be overshadowed by poor feature usability. And the business world factors of time and budget must always be part of the balance; they often require abandoning aspects of the best long-term design. But it's very important to balance *them* with the fact that, in the long run, users think of the product more than the time or money taken to produce it. Regardless of the exact priorities and the resulting design decisions, it is extremely beneficial to specifically document each potential system variable that was identified but designed constant; this definitely saves on later *repeat analyzing*. All of this facilitates the continually simplest design, which provides the total identified functionality.

In any designing situation, it is extremely beneficial to specifically document each potential system variable that was identified but designed constant; this definitely saves on later *repeat analyzing*.

LOW-LEVEL DESIGNING WITH C++

C++ has a feature that enables a single set of code to be applied to multiple classes (one at a time), at compile time. This feature is called a **template**, and it is, essentially, a text substituter. But it's part of the compiler, not a *pre*compiler, so it's built around (data) type checking, which makes it a little more sophisticated—essentially, it's *interactive* with data types. Combined with multiple inheritance, this aspect makes it possible for templates to be used as a *basis* for code generation.

Just as objects are frequently bound to each other at execution time through parameters, templates can be used to actually bind *classes* to each other at *compile* time through layered *template* parameters. This ability, then, brings binding up another level. The layers and the interactive evaluation by the compiler cause *recursive substitution*. Combining specifically compatible types of templates and classes causes recursive substitution, which leads to a wide range of compiler-generated code.

As is so often the case with C++, this type of effort is a world of its own.

Very Broad Philosophy

With reference to the growth in comprehension from programming to designing, function orientation is the next step of growth. Obviously, there is the factor of consideration of the reoriented structure, but the much more prevalent consideration is of the sophisticated interaction mechanisms, which causes function-oriented designing to entail a thorough understanding of characteristics of systems in general and how to best manage them. This results in a mental collection of *multidimensional patterns*.

A further dimension of designing includes the understanding of how multiple instances of the same class concurrently access the same persistent object collections. This applies to mostly instances that are managed by other classes' objects. But it can also apply to instances that are managed by like objects; these instances are **threads**. (Threads are treated as a fundamental concept in Java.) In some situations, an entire collection must be updated exclusively by one object, so multiple concurrent threads are not possible then; these are for deletion, sorting, and backup (because backups are physical, not logical)—basically, when a whole-file snapshot is needed. All of this is multiplied in a time-sharing environment, including a multitasking stand-alone computer and, even more, a server.

And there are bigger ramifications of function-oriented designing strategies than just the software. Software systems parallel the business processes they are accommodating. Software design experts are, more broadly, process design experts, and they should apply their efforts to the business processes, as thoroughly as is reasonable, to benefit the business, as much as possible. They can leverage the lower cost of the resultant software (in addition to that of the business processes themselves) against any resistance to change.

Specifically, function-oriented designing is geared to long-term (overall) benefits, which is good guidance for business. And the guidance of function set integrity is also good for business processes; here, violation of business function set (business group) integrity should be seen as a last resort. Further, the appropriateness of function orientation being applied directly to business processes is supported by a common parallel and extension to function orientation, which is the *encapsulation of business logic*—separation from the user interface and data store—in a design known as **3-tier architecture**.

All of this requires extensive designing effort to ensure that the resultant systems are as effective as possible and, at the very least, not chaotic. There is often pressure from business managers to start programming and produce as much functionality as possible quickly, but, of course, that is contrary to the fact that the design is the most important thing. In these instances, it can be pointed out that *designing is management, and programming without strong designing is like operation without strong management*. The extra beauty here is that managers who tend to push harder understand this better.

And the most direct balance between design and business needs is in the most crucial analysis questioning. It's in the ongoing discussions about the project scope that come from the recursive, narrowing, designing efforts. It's crucial to have a reasonable scope of what capabilities the software will have, in what order (and in what versions) and in what time frame. These are, ultimately, integral aspects of the environment of the software.

In any software development, but perhaps particularly in function-oriented software development, people who are strongly guided by its underlying philosophies—people who are best able to teach, to many audiences—tend to be more integral and rarer than people who "know" a particular technology. They are the ones who are best able to apply the most effective development practices to every aspect, and every member, of the effort.

General Recommendation

Of course, a significant issue in any project is how long it takes to complete. And, of course, *predictions* of how long it will take are directly related. When predictions are substantially low, they tend to cause undue pressure, extreme stress, poor communication, severe mistakes, runaway finger-pointing, and pervasive burnout. And inaccurate predictions are fueled by a lack of relevant statistics, especially when a set of technologies is new to a company, and even more when the technologies themselves are new.

All of this is combatted with continually updated project actuarial tables. One *very* useful type can be compiled with statistics from projects across many companies, which can remain *anonymous*, as general standards. The other type is compiled by each company for itself, with statistics from its projects, to account for its individual combination of circumstances and to allow self-monitoring against the standards. This effort provides for highly educated guesses.

■ ■ ■

CHAPTER THREE

Untangled Web
The Evolution of an Enterprise-Level Design

This chapter lays out relationships among user and storage interfaces, and some of their implementations in various computer environments.

Overall Processing Flows

Comprehensively understanding a piece of software begins with understanding its overall processing flow. And that begins with the overall flow of its user request processing. This is made much clearer by examination of the history of approaches.

Keyboard-Only Interaction

The keyboard alone actually had grown to have many interaction capabilities.

Interfaces

Human Interaction

What time do you have?

Set your clock to 12:34:56.

The ability of a person to just type letters, numbers, and punctuation characters into a computer most obviously leads to interacting with it, to get it to *do* things, by typing sentences—of commands, with subjects and (grammatical) objects, and prepositions between them, and complete punctuation. A variation of this is asking it questions. Generically, commands and questions are **directives**.

But that most obvious, most direct approach can easily become much too wordy. And part of any progress is more efficiency. Toward that, the most direct derivative of typing a sentence is skipping much of the punctuation and the prepositions; obviously, this is no longer a sentence. And this easily leads to just a *statement* of the desired result; many directives are statements. One common example of this is the directive "TIME", which states that the user wants a report of the current time. "TIME value" states that the user wants the time to be set.

The next most obvious derivative is abbreviating the words to varying degrees—creating codes. Then, it's helpful to leave the full words as options, for clarity, especially for people who haven't used the computer before—because, at a glance, this interaction is no longer very person-friendly (**user-friendly**). What it is, however, is the standard form of interaction that existed for much of the history of computers.

Directives in this scheme are typed in response to a generic prompt, which varies by program. The placeholder for all of this interaction—the thing that lets the user know where the typing will occur on the screen—is the **cursor**.

Formatted Guidance

```
Customer Administration Menu

   A   Add a Customer
   C   Change a Customer's Info
   D   Delete a Customer

Please choose an option: ▓
```

Toward user-friendliness, another interaction that became standard is specifically prompting the user for pieces of information that they don't include in their directive. Further along this line is listing available directives, with a code for each, and prompting the user for a code, especially formatting this as a *display*, using the coordinates of the screen; this is the first version of a **menu**. From a different direction, providing **help** text—a noninteractive explanation of directive capabilities—also became standard. Another move toward user-friendliness, from another different direction, is allowing the user to specify codes to be interpreted as directives, on an ongoing basis; one name for this is **aliases**.

A directive can put the computer into a different interaction **mode**. This means that the computer will then handle pieces of information in a different way. Actually, sometimes what has happened is that the directive has started another program. It's often reflected in changes of prompt. So, even the same word can mean different things in different modes. In more user-friendly terms, a mode is really a context.

The next efficiency derivative is creating specific keys to be used in combination with the typewriter keys—the letters, numbers, and punctuation—as an alternative to typing codes. This is especially efficient when the directive is for a different mode; otherwise, two directives would have to be made: one to change the mode and one for the desired directive.

The next derivative of *this* is creating specific keys to be the equivalent of combinations of other keys, for **one-touch** directives. Each of these keys holds a *sequence* of characters. This is what a function key (F-key) is. Actually, nearly *all* of the extra (nontypewriter) keys are sequence keys. The further derivative of this is inserting a level of indirection, logically attaching a sequence *to a directive* (or pieces of information, or multiple directives), which the user can specify. This can be done directly by the user or by recording keystrokes.

Finally, a move toward both efficiency and user-friendliness is a **form**—placing (and labeling) several types of information on the screen at the same time. It can be interactive or noninteractive with the computer. The interactive form is processed one field at a time, as the field is entered; the noninteractive form requires *submission* of the entire form to interact with the computer.

A form is the most extensive use of screen coordinates. Effectively, it also allows several modes to be addressed at the same time. Actually, it enables the equivalent of several directives at the same time, all prompted. A form has a degree of putting the user in control of the interaction.

Formatted Selection

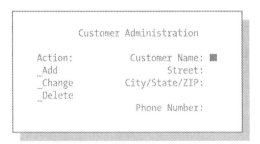

Also, a form allows specifying choices from lists of available options, for example, by typing an "X" next to them. And a form can have a menu right on it; if there's not enough space for that, it can list a key or directive that displays the menu.

So, even a nongraphic configuration can be made very user-friendly—very clear all along the way.

Implementations

Direct interaction with prompts is caused by a program—operating system (OS) or application—reading from the screen. The program could have immediately preceded the read with a display of the prompt, or it could have displayed the prompt previously and placed the cursor appropriately.

The most direct processing of the read text is evaluation and branching, with successive conditional tests, and error messages for any text that doesn't meet all of the requirements the program has for a directive in the current context. This is an example of the processes of a **command interpreter**.

As relatively advanced an interface as a form is, the interactive implementation is as simple as moving the cursor from field to field, handling each directly. The noninteractive implementation entails mapping the fields to a set of variables and handling the set, addressing the variables in any order.

More-indirect processing by a program is possible with some automatic processing, most likely provided by the compiler. One example of this is that a piece of code can be named a specific way to be automatically branched to when a corresponding key is pressed. A fourth-generation version involves another level of indirection: it allows code to be named in any way but requires the key to be assigned to that name.

On an interactive computer, a very different implementation, **keystroke processing**, has a very straightforward name. It processes one keystroke at a time, allowing any key to direct any process. In normal interactive mode, the *system* will automatically send each typewriter key to that user's screen; this is **echoing**. Echoing can be turned off; a good reason to do this is for password entry. Also, the normal configuration requires a **delimiter** key—for example, a Return, Enter, or F-key—for the program to receive the text.

In keystroke processing mode, the *program* receives each key; it doesn't require a delimiter. There is no automatic echoing; the program itself does the echoing, most simply by just displaying the pressed key at the current location of the cursor. But, again, the program can do anything with any key. A simple example of this is that it can monitor the position of the cursor on its line and, when needed, find the farthest-right space, blank-out back to it, and display the current word on the next line. This is the process of **text wrapping**.

Reliable Keystroke Processing

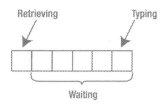

Retrieving   Typing

Waiting

Because some processes take longer than it takes to type successive keys, reliable keystroke processing also requires **keystroke pooling**. This is a level of indirection; the program *monitors* the pool. It checks the pool for characters. If any are there, it reads one and processes that, by evaluation and branching. Then it checks again; so, this processing is in a *cycle*. It is also an example of indirection between interaction and processing. (And it's what allows type-ahead entry.)

Visual Object Interaction

The capabilities of forms were greatly expanded by GUIs. Pixels were harnessed with the creation of the free-moving pointer—and the **mouse**. This enabled more types of interaction—so, also more formats of the same directive—more *intuitive* interaction, and nearly random control by the user.

However, to serve productivity, many people who are fluid on the keyboard prefer to keep both hands set in one place—in the typewriter position—or as close to it as possible, so they like to use the mouse as little as possible. A couple of modifications to the design of the separate side mouse place a roller ball or a flat roller pad below the spacebar, allowing pointer movement with either thumb, without moving the hands.

Even with the older design, a strategy compensates for there being so many extra keys on the right side of the keyboard. Placing the mouse on the left side (and reversing the operations of the left and right buttons) eliminates having to reach so far for the mouse, enabling both hands to stay as close to one place as possible. This is simply an example of both hands being more productive than just one.

Interfaces

These are very familiar, but it's useful to run down this range of interactions in a specific way.

The simplest interaction through a mouse is the ability to **point and click**—to point to something on the screen and click on it. Related to the keyboard, the simplest use of this is to point at some text and click to move the cursor to that point. This ability is standard in any text entry area of the screen.

The way to show available directives closest to the keyboard version is to click on **drop-down menu** headers. This design allows several menus to be viewed at nearly the same time and, so, for a single partitioned menu to be separated into multiple simple menus. The pointer can then be dragged down any of the menus to *select* a directive.

But, of course, the ability to click on a picture or symbol of something—an **icon**—is a prominent benefit of pixels. One use of an icon is as a piece of information; clicking on the icon *selects* it, putting that information into *focus*, making it the subject of applicable menu directives. It's easy to see that moving a cursor is actually an example of setting a focus.

For another use, an icon makes an available directive more immediately obvious, which generally makes the user more comfortable. And, of course, *double-clicking* on an icon is the equivalent of entering a directive. For example, double-clicking on a data file directs to open it with its default application, and double-clicking on an application directs to open a new (or default) data file with that application.

The next operation related to the keyboard is the ability to point at one position in some text and *drag* to another position, to select all of the text in between (putting it into focus). This can be applied to selecting multiple icons, as well.

The ability to **drag and drop**—to drag a selection into another position on the screen (in an icon or some text)—represents a directive to move (or copy) an item. It can also represent a **focus and direct**—at the same time setting the focus and directing something on it, like opening with a specific application or printing to a specific printer.

The GUI version of a form has the same features as the keyboard-only version, enhanced from the ability to point and click. Text entry fields have the standard editing features; multiple-option lists have small **buttons** with two appearances, one for single- and another for multiple-*choice*. A GUI form also provides much more visual variety. For example, choice from a range can also be represented by a sliding box on a horizontal or vertical bar, or up and down arrows next to a number. A complex form can also be partitioned into a categorized multiform, in which only one category is visible at a time; this is typically represented by some arrangement of **tabs**, each with short text.

One of a GUI's functions is to provide visual variety.

A form also has large processing buttons, typically at any edge, for the user to, for example, submit or cancel the information on the form; these are labeled most often with short text. So, a GUI form has both interactive and noninteractive features. (The ability to cancel is extremely helpful, because it allows a lot of free exploration of options. This is similar to the extremely helpful ability to *undo* multiple directives, which isn't a *visual* interaction.) And, of course, anything on a form can also have an icon.

Adapting the usage of buttons, the most frequently used directives of menus can be made permanently visible in the form of a **toolbar** or a **palette**, which shows each directive as a button, most often with a picture. These are also much more compact than menus.

Finally, multiple concurrent interactions with each application are viewable because of the ability to show multiple, sometimes overlapping, windows on the same screen. Compared to the keyboard-only environment, this is like one user having multiple screens.

The GUI version of prompting is in a **dialog**, which is really a type of form that pops up and must be processed before concurrent interactions with that application can be continued. Typically, a dialog has a prompt message and processing buttons. Sometimes it needs a text-entry field, but usually the prompt has simple options, so the processing buttons on a dialog serve the same purpose as single-choice buttons on a normal form.

Implementations

The implementations of visual object interfaces are much the same as keyboard-only implementations, combined in different ways and enhanced for the ability to point and click.

Painting—placement and appearance—of visual objects, and direct interaction with them, are managed by the GUI's run-time system. This is crucial, because these are very complex, and very standard, operations. The run-time system (RTS) *interprets* the user's actions, based on locations of mouse clicks and so on, and passes this to the application, so this is a level of indirection. This context sees the user's directives as **events**.

One way to connect the interpretation to the application is to pool the interpretations and have the application monitor the pool, in a cycle. The application then processes one user directive at a time, by evaluation and branching, to event handling code. This is much like the key processing design.

Because the monitoring cycle is a standard process (protocol) and, therefore, not a case of ultimate control by the application, a better way to implement it is to shift it to the RTS. Here, the RTS is programmatically called to **register** each piece of handling code. This accomplishes the same processing as the keyboard-only approach, but it doesn't require fourth generation. In this configuration, the handling code is an **observer** (also commonly called a **listener**) of the event. With many languages that allow addressing of individual functions, this technique has the RTS handling all of the branching, which allows programmers to focus the most on the applications. (Ironically, Java doesn't have this level of function orientation.)

A fairly obvious practicality is to handle visual objects with code objects, one class for each type. In fact, this was one of the first widely accepted uses of object orientation. While it's not *required* for GUIs, some of which have operated on just protocols, this approach has fundamental benefits, built on organization, quick repeatability, and integrated flexibility.

The organization is on multiple levels. The branching services of the RTS become gathered into a type of class that is in control of the other types of classes involved; this type is easily named a **controller**. The painting-and-interpretation services become a type of class that the user interacts with directly; it's called a **view**. And the application, which is based on and serves the practical functions the user wants the computer to perform, is called a **model**. Together, the mechanism is commonly referred to as **Model-View-Controller** (**MVC**), which is an example of the Mediator mechanism type.

Overlapping Views of the 3-Tier Design

Presentation	Presentation Server	Core	Storage Server	Storage
View	Controller	Model	Middleware	Legacy System

Mediator

In the context of the 3-tier design, MVC deals with the presentation and core tiers, with the controller as a level of indirection. To draw a parallel to a storage server, the controller can be seen as a presentation server. Overall, then, the 3-tier design is really of three *primary* tiers connected through two *secondary* tiers.

Each visual object can be created quickly through instantiation of the corresponding class. Its personal values include its location on the form, size, label text, color, and previous corresponding user directive.

And, with the run-time system organized into standard classes, *it* can even be functionally extended, *to tailor it* in various ways, to the applications. It's fairly easy to see that the standard classes approach has many of the same features as the fourth-generation approach, but it's more flexible. The process of calling the classes as desired puts programmers in much more control, and the ability to choose and combine classes allows functionally creating multiple fourth-generation environments. (And this supports the earlier clarification that standard-class systems are usually toolkits. Fourth-generation systems are closer to frameworks.)

The ability to choose and combine classes allows functionally creating multiple fourth-generation environments.

So, object orientation provides very efficient harnessing of extensive, standardized user interface processing.

Network Browsers

A browser is just a user presentation device for information sent over a network—the internet or an intranet.

Just Text and Pictures

The core capabilities of a browser are just to display fairly simply formatted text and pictures, and allow some of these to be clicked on to display other text and pictures. This is one *page* at a time, though one page can be *very* long, and the clickable elements have a *link* to another page (or another part of the same page). A network *site*, commonly referred to as a website, typically has multiple pages; a linked page can be in the same or a different site. And any page can be displayed by a statement, but this type of statement can be anywhere from *fairly* cryptic to *very* cryptic. These capabilities comprise the entire core interface.

A network browser is essentially its own run-time system, just for presentation. There is no compiler related to this RTS; everything is directly interpreted. A browser's main function is to efficiently format a stream of text and picture files which that text references.

The text is marked at various points with combinations of directive elements (**tags**) that indicate how it should be formatted.

The tags are of HyperText Markup Language (HTML), which is designed specifically for browsers. Each browser page comes from an HTML **document**. HTML is an application of a framework for markup languages; Standard Generalized Markup Language (SGML) is a metalanguage, and any SGML-based language requires an SGML Document Type Definition (DTD). (Other SGML languages are used for the more-complex formats of things like word processing documents.)

Most HTML tags exist in pairs: one is the beginning tag, and the other is the ending tag, and they affect the text between them. Lone tags indicate one or more nontext characters. Each tag is enclosed in angle brackets: `<` and `>`. Each ending tag has the same directive as its beginning tag, preceded by a slash; for example, `<b>` and `</b>` direct the text between them to be formatted bold. Comment tags are the exception; for a comment, the beginning tag is `<!--` and the ending tag is `-->`. When it's appropriate, beginning and ending tags can be combined, by ending the beginning tag with the slash. For example, some tags have parameters (**attributes**); one beginning-and-ending tag is `<img src="file" alt="text" />`. There are multiple browsers, and any browser can have its own tags that are not part of HTML.

HTML tags are short (abbreviations), because they were designed to be easily entered manually. But, in the context of user (developer)-friendly development tools, which are the standard for older (more mature) technologies, the tagged-text code configuration is very primitive. There are (fairly immature) tools that interpret from *and to* HTML, but they often create documents that are difficult to read manually or that have numerous unnecessary tags, so hand coding is still the standard.

Browsers themselves can interpret only text, tags, and pictures. These fairly straightforward elements don't require programmers; they're actually most effectively developed by *authors* and *graphic artists*. But even this development can have some complexity; for example, because it takes longer to load (receive and format) graphics than text, to maximize viewers' interest, it's common to display the page in stages (saving complex graphics for last) and display graphics with a fade-in effect from a graphics editor. Differently complex is presenting multiple pages at the same time, one in each explicitly defined section (**frame**) of the display.

Browsers also provide a separation between page content and its appearance, making HTML documents easier to maintain, with the ability to keep collections of formats in one or more of their own specialized documents. They have their own syntax, which has more extensive control of formats than does HTML, and one of these documents can reference others. A collection of formats is a **style** (similar to that of a word processor), the dedicated documents are called **sheets**, and the recursive referencing is called **cascading**—this is the feature of Cascading Style Sheets (CSS). Because of CSS, HTML format attributes are officially discouraged.

But *exact* formatting differs among browsers, in multiple ways, of various significances. So, there is a fundamental lack of control by internet site developers, as they can't be sure that their pages will appear as they intend. Browsers identify themselves upon request, so tags can be changed for each; this process is **polling**, for a browser's overall or individual capabilities. Thorough internet testing includes using multiple browsers. But users can also alter formatting options on the same browser, so even in*tra*net presentation can't be completely relied on by developers.

The cryptic statements and the links, which are these statements embedded in **anchor** (`<a>`) tags, are each a Uniform Resource Locater (URL). This has the streamed Uniform Resource Identifier (URI) syntax, which has multiple parts. A URL is commonly referred to as a **web address**.

BASIC URI SYNTAX

The main part of a URL statement is the **domain** reference. The domain holds the implementation of the site. The reference can be an **Internet Protocol** (**IP**) **address**, which refers to the location of a site server, or a **domain name**, which refers to an IP address. A domain name is more commonly used, because it typically describes the general content of the site—for example, a company name or product name. Names are also more useful for two other reasons: one server can have multiple domains, and a domain can be moved from server to server without having to change its name. Assignment of addresses and names is governed by various **registry** organizations. Both the IP address and domain name also have parts.

- An IP address is commonly four numbers separated by periods; each of these is from 0 to 255. The internet is a multileveled connection of computers, so it's easy to think that each of the numbers corresponds to a level, but it doesn't. It's actually a representation of a 32-bit number—an integer, from 0 to $2^{32}-1$ (which is over 4 billion); this is simply the key for the location information. Each IP address number is just the decimal equivalent of eight of the bits. (A 128-bit number is proposed. Its representation would be up to 8 four-digit hexadecimal numbers [16 bits], separated by colons.)

- A domain name *does* have levels, separated by periods; however, these are in reverse order. For example, in `www.apress.com`, `com` is the top level, and `apress` is the second level. `www` is technically the subdomain, which is actually a reminder that the web is a subset of the internet. A name is translated to an IP address (**resolved**) by the Domain Name System (DNS), which is managed by the Internet Corporation for Assigned Names and Numbers (ICANN).

Before the domain reference, the URL indicates the data transfer method—the **transfer protocol**. This is most often the HyperText Transfer Protocol (HTTP). The protocol is represented in lowercase, followed by a colon and separated from the domain name by a double slash. For example, `http://www.apress.com` is a minimum URL. This is the site's default address, and it locates the main (**home**) page of the site.

A page is specified following the domain name, separated by a single slash; the document name's default extension is `.html`. Further, the default page is `default.html`; so, for the previous Apress home address, `http://www.apress.com/default.html` is implied.

Sites, and therefore their pages, can be nested in a hierarchic directory structure. Each additional level is simply denoted by the directory name and a further slash preceding the document name. This forms a **path**.

A link to a (named) element of a page is the last part, preceded by a number sign—#. It's actually not part of the URL, but a reference that is held by the browser just for page positioning.

The processing flow is as follows. The browser sends the URL directives to the located server, and the server sends the document's streamed text and referenced picture files back to the browser. This type of HTML document server is commonly called a **web server**; for example, one well-known web server is Tomcat. Both of these occur through the transfer protocol, the IP address information, and the server's directory structure (through its OS). So, it's fairly easy to see that this combination has the functionality of a controller, the browser is a view, and the documents are a model.

Added Interaction and Manageability

Pages benefit greatly from added interaction. For example, visual effects that vary with a user's movement of the mouse provide instant feedback—and also keep the user's attention. These are the things that gave browsers more interaction capabilities than any other configuration. Also, form fields for entry of information, simple editing functionality for form entries, and window effects including pop-up messages allow a *user* to provide specific feedback. And all of this can be tailored to the user's preferences and previous activities.

The mouse-sensitive visual effects are accommodated with extra attributes on the image tag. For form fields—the browser version of the GUI components—browsers just have additional tags with identification attributes. The new tags and attributes are still reasonably developed by nonprogrammers (authors and artists).

But the more complex processing, and organized control of all of these features, is beyond the capabilities of the tagged-text configuration. Giving a browser the ability to interpret a limited-programming (**script**) language mixed into the document, along with requiring the browser to create and maintain an organized representation of every component it presents, adds these capabilities. This configuration handles everything a browser now does directly besides format text, tags, and pictures, and send URLs. But it also requires a level of programming skill.

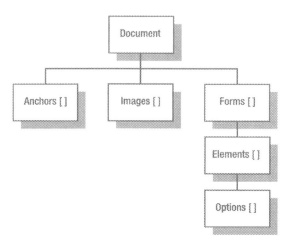

Partial Document Object Model

The first language for this has the basic syntax of Java. It was originally called LiveScript, to reflect its immediate effects, but its name was quickly changed to JavaScript, to reflect its similar programming feel. JavaScript was created by Netscape; its name was created through an agreement with Sun.

And the organized representation of document components is in the form of a standardized multilevel aggregation of objects called the Document Object Model (DOM). The ability to manipulate the DOM is what gives JavaScript control of the browser's presentation. Through the DOM, JavaScript can set any component, down to the attribute level. So, for example, JavaScript can change the CSS style assigned to any group of components.

The DOM accommodates user actions as various events; each of these has a corresponding tag attribute. JavaScript can be set as the attribute value in response to the event. For processing during the (noninteractive) loading of the page, JavaScript requires its own script tag pair (`<script language="Javascript">` and `</script>`). Any piece of JavaScript code can be kept in its own file and referenced with the script tag's additional `src` attribute.

JavaScript also has timing (automatic) events, which allow it to change the presentation *without* user interaction. This literally animates the presentation, including allowing videos. Some tools (like Flash) separate this capability into a configuration that provides management focused on it. These are graphics *players*; they are implemented as separate browser extensions (**plug-ins**). A player is actually a graphics *sequencer*, which displays a series of graphics in succession (very quickly). Some have controls for actions like pausing and rewinding.

Also, a specialized type of file accommodates parameters and values, for storing things like user settings and activities across site visits. This type of file is called a **cookie**, which also fits the Java naming scheme.

Combining of HTML, CSS, and JavaScript is a *technique* often called **dynamic HTML** (**DHTML**). But it's very important to understand that this technique enables changing what *pieces* of a document are presented, based on various criteria; in other words, besides window control, JavaScript provides only *dynamic selection of static content.*

JavaScript provides dynamic *selection* of static content.

Network Site Servers

The bulk of a network site application—most of all three tiers—is on the server. This degree of implementation in site development requires high-level programming.

The following subsections describe various aspects of the server environment.

More Java

Java was designed to accommodate networks, with fundamental object orientation. Because of the diversity of computers in a network, Java was designed to be extremely portable. And, because a transmitted application can introduce powerful functionality into another computer, Java was also designed on fundamental security.

Java can be in a class with a main function, for standard desktop (GUI) applications. The most direct initiation of this is through the OS command line, with the `java` directive. It's likewise compiled with the `javac` directive. The programming-language (source) class file's extension is `.java`, and the compiled class file's extension is `.class`.

Java Compilation Configuration

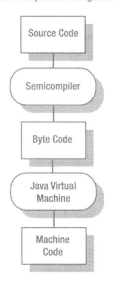

Actually, the `.class` code isn't really compiled; it's *semi*compiled. Java's run-time system does the rest of the compilation. This approach was taken specifically to allow one Java program to easily be run on multiple operating systems—any OS that has a Java RTS. This is, therefore, a one-to-many relationship. Java calls its semicompiled code **byte code** and the core of its RTSs, a **Java Virtual Machine** (**JVM**). A **Java Runtime** also has the Java standard classes.

(Microsoft adapted the approach in the opposite direction, to serve just its OS. It semicompiles both C# and Visual Basic [VB] into the same code [**Intermediate Language**] and has one RTS [the **Common Language Runtime**]. So, this is a many-to-one relationship, and it's how C# and VB have nearly identical functionality, just with differing syntax.)

Java code can be included throughout a final (client-side) document, without a main function, and presented in its own logical GUI frame. This is handled by the browser, indirectly, with a plug-in. In essence, each piece of Java code is a mini-application, so it's called an **applet**; this approach requires extension of the `Applet` class (from the `java.applet` package). And the browser is the direct RTS for the applet; it is commonly seen as a context or a **container** for the applet. There has never been much use made of applets, but the same approach can be applied to the server side, and this is *widely* used.

Java code can be in a class that is handled by a dedicated server-side container, as a mini-application; this version is a **servlet**. A servlet has more functionality than an applet, so it must extend one of *multiple* classes. There's one class for each of the common transfer protocols, derived from the abstract `Servlet` class. For example, HTTP processing is handled by the `HttpServlet` class. All of these are under the `javax.servlet` package; the `x` is for extension (to the original Java standard packages).

Servlets can add any programming capability to a site application. One use for this is to allow users to buy things the site is displaying—because sites do very often exist to advertise a company or a product. This interaction is **e-commerce**. The connections between a container and the servlets it executes are dynamic, so a servlet can be recompiled without having to recompile (and restart) the container; this feature has the same effect as sending an applet in a document. Servlet and other server-side containers are typically part of an **application server**; one well-known application server is JBoss.

Again, any programming language is designed to accommodate a point of view. Just a couple of other examples of how Java accommodates the needs of site processing involve its handling of multiple levels of variables and multiple users of logic-sensitive resources.

There are collections of variables for each *page*, *request* (which can process across multiple pages), *session* (for one user's multiple requests), and *application* (for all users). Each level is called a variable **scope**, and Java represents them in objects from standard classes. It also has a collection for each response. In addition, access commands have been created for these in JavaScript.

In the multiple-user environment of a server, Java's threads must be made to not adversely affect each other's processing; this is **thread safety**. One way to accomplish this is to prevent concurrent updates of an object, which makes one access wait until others are finished, through an internal list (queue). The approach is called **synchronization**, and it simply (program) scopes the access code with `synchronized (object) {code}`. (Further, access to any *primitive* variable can be synchronized by the technique of making it an array of one occurrence first. This works because an array of primitives is an object.)

In the absence of synchronization, a protocol can ensure thread safety. For example, the servlet container calls the `init()` and `destroy()` functions at the start and finish of the servlet's processing, respectively. Each servlet can be shared by many users, so the servlet protocol requires that updates occur in only these functions.

Storage Interaction

The other end of the 3-tier configuration has the secondary tier of the database connection. There are standardized services for this, provided by standard classes. Java's implementation is Java Database Connectivity (JDBC). It incorporates indirection to allow one type of functional data to be moved from one type of database to another; the indirection sees the direct entity simply as a **data source**.

Establishing a connection to the database entails a lot of standard processing overhead, so it should be done as little as possible. JDBC's configuration also allows database connections to be preserved and just assigned and unassigned to application processes as needed. This is called **connection pooling**.

As was mentioned earlier in the book, this processing makes the most sense in a dedicated *data object*.

Preprocessing for Variability

For thorough practicality, pages need *fundamental* variability. There are many uses for this. For example, if pages' information gets updated regularly, if appropriate information varies by request, and if users should be able to customize their interaction—all of these call for being able to change pages automatically. This is **dynamic content**.

Because browsers can handle only static content, dynamic processing must *generate* static content before the browser processes it. This occurs on the server's side. Request responses are actually interrupted by multiple preprocessors, which have their turn in a particular order, administered by the server.

Dynamic processing must *generate* static content, on the server's side, before the browser processes it.

Dynamic processing can occur implicitly, for any preset conditions. Also, requests can explicitly initiate a dynamic process. A URL can have parameters following the document name. The first is preceded by a question mark, and then multiple parameters are separated by an ampersand: `&`.

Through servlets, Java can output HTML to a file that is then sent to the browser. This is the actual (internal) process of fourth generation. So, servlets can drive the entire presentation, whether based on execution conditions or not. But, clearly, this configuration doesn't satisfy the separation of presentation and core processing into MVC.

Variable Markup

HTML has a standard set of tags designed for a single set of purposes. The technique of tagging is good for formatting any data from a stream of characters and the reverse—converting formatted data into a stream, which is called **serialization**. These tags, then, are used to describe (define) the data. And the tags must be tailored to each set of data.

This is the purpose of eXtensible Markup Language (XML). So, XML is another *meta-*language; it's actually a subset of SGML. Because there are innumerable sets of data, and because this formatting requires only associating values with data items (and data items with each other), XML is specifically designed to enable simpler definition of markup languages.

XML is a subset of the SGML *meta*language, specifically designed to enable simpler definition of markup languages.

But XML's fundamental flexibility must be anchored by a strict syntax structure. Every beginning tag must have an ending tag, and combined tag scopes must create a solid structure—properly stacked. In other words, a scope that contains another scope can't logically end before that (contained) one. These rules are said to create **well-formed** definitions. (SGML has these same rules *and alternatives*.) So, XML can be used to very effectively define *data structures*.

XML tags are typically spelled out and easily understandable, as program variable names are. Just as with HTML, an ending tag is the same as its beginning tag, preceded by a slash. And, for human readability, the data definitions are typically indented to reflect the structures, like an outline; this is very helpful, because an XML document can become extremely wordy.

XML SYNTAX REVISION

Actually, given the strict structure, the rules can very reasonably be changed to make XML much more readable. Specifically, the ending tags, each indented in direct relation to its beginning tag, don't further need the same name trailing the slash. Any ending tag can be just < / >; this is similar to just the right brace scope ender in Java. Minimized ending tags also speed up reading by the computer (**parsing**), which is noticeably slow.

The structure-based definition document is (arguably) even more readable breaking with the right brace tradition of alignment directly under the beginning position of the scope definer, by lining up the ending tag under the beginning position of the indented elements. This causes beginning tags to stand out more, making any definition easier to manually find, especially in very large XML documents, which are common.

(In many contexts, commitment to old syntax can be very limiting. Revised syntax incorporates lessons of usage, to *facilitate* usage. Actually, it can be seen that new syntax is commitment to old syntax, with a level of indirection.)

The standard document for tag definition went from XML's version of Document Type Definition, with DTD language, to XML Schema, with the more appropriately capable eXtensible Stylesheet Language (XSL).

XML's narrowing of syntax rules is applied to HTML as the XHTML language.

And it's sometimes useful to format XML data items for presentation on a browser. Translation from an XML language to XHTML is accommodated by a facility called XSL Transformation (XSLT), which is made up of standard classes.

Application Management

One use of XML that is very useful in development is assigning values to class (program) data items. This enables changing values within a class without the need to recompile. But it requires a level of indirection in the programming, using an XML parser in the class, instead of a simple assignment. This actually has the same feel as assignment through user input; in this case, the user is a developer. Many third-party toolkits and frameworks use this approach.

A use of the value assignment capability is assigning file names to an application's file name variables. In XML, file names can be relative to the application's (base) path, which is frequently called a **context**. Class names can even be assigned to class name variables, in a sequence, assigning values to parameters for each of these. All of this is the functionality of a much older technology dedicated to just this purpose: IBM's Job Control Language (JCL). In XML, it's a **configuration file**, and it's enabled by an XML parse and then a reflection-based instantiation. Many third-party frameworks use this to enable extensions (plug-ins).

The configuration file approach has the further capability of using multiple same-level variables to represent a connection. Most powerfully, multiple same-level class variables can establish a dependence. Under a higher-level variable, these can establish a collection (aggregation) or a composition.

It's fairly easy to see that all of these are examples of functional controller extension.

XML documents of these types facilitate analysis of entire applications and their structures. A configuration file especially serves as a *road map* for large applications, which are common.

XML documents can extend control and facilitate analysis of entire applications.

Automated Programming Management

As opposed to toolkits used by developers *in* application processes, XML is also leveraged in toolkits that are used by developers for application *development* processes. Two examples are for compiling and testing.

There's a third-party Java tool based on the C tool called Make. Make facilitates managing resources for compilations. This small but powerful Java tool is appropriately called **Ant**. Ant was created to manage resources for compilations and be portable (to any computer with a Java Runtime), but it was also built in such a way that it could be fairly easily extended. It uses XML-style tags for user (developer) control over its actions, with a specific type of tag it calls a **task**. Each task has a corresponding Java class; this is instead of a schema, because each of these tags represents more than just data structuring. And creating a new task simply requires creating one of these classes, so many third-party tasks have been created, and Ant is also used to create collections of compiled classes—Java ARchive (JAR) files—and run other third-party tools.

Java has a very simple self-contained feature that is used for unit (class) testing, to *assert* a presumed state at that point in the execution and cause an error if the "assertion" is incorrect. There is a third-party tool that executes classes and compares assertion results with previous results, generating an identifying message when they don't match; this tool is called **JUnit**. Specific Ant tasks for integrating JUnit testing into the compilation process create thoroughly automated testing.

Storage Interaction with a New Subcontext

Some storage server software has been extended to include serving XML.

Taking a step back, it's fairly easy to see that the XML tagged-data design is *data mixed with metadata, for every instance* of the data. It's specifically designed to *directly interpret data through a text transfer protocol that has no infrastructure for that*. It eliminates the need for extra references (to metadata), for each instance of interpretation of the data. Outside of that purpose, other configurations are more practical. Especially, XML is efficiently hand-coded for only *very* low counts of instances; for higher counts to be handled well, XML needs the additional capabilities of processing tags separated from data and applying a single set of those tags to multiple instances of data.

Independently, compared with a relational database—of each level of a data structure placed in a separate table—*XML is data in its extracted form*, a logical *cross* view that *combines* (joins) the tables appropriately. Extracted data has repetitions of the same instance of one level referenced by multiple instances of another level. It, therefore, is significantly larger than the separated form and can require repetition to make a single change—which also makes data integrity more difficult to maintain. These are the reasons for the database configuration in the first place.

Obviously, XML and relational databases have two differing major purposes.

XML is data in its extracted form, mixed with metadata, to directly interpret the data through a text transfer protocol that has no infrastructure for that.

Just for perspective, XML can most efficiently be applied to represent tables with additional tags for generic table structures—for column *properties*—if these are the only structures in the representation. In many cases, though, all of the structures must be read for any single data item to be reliably interpreted, so it couldn't be *directly* parsed. This indicates that the only real use for this configuration is temporary conversion from one database to another.

Standardized Objects

To facilitate tools that create GUIs, to allow them to easily identify a GUI object class's functionality, the Java community designed creation of standardized objects by combining classes with a protocol. In a GUI creation tool, a GUI object is referred to simply as a **component**. And the result of Java's design is a **JavaBean**.

The protocol has three groups of standards: one each for instantiation, access, and persistence. First, a JavaBean requires a no-argument constructor; it can have other constructors as well, but it must have (at least the interface of) a constructor that takes no parameters. Second, it must have getters and setters for its object-level data items (**properties**); it must have a function whose name begins with "set" for the update of each property, and one whose name begins with "get" (or "is" for a Boolean item) for the report of its value. Third, the Bean must be serializable (convertible to XML). It must implement either the Serializable or Externalizable interface (in the java.io package).

And visual developer classes are also typically composed of visual standard objects. Because these standardized classes are designed specifically to be managed by tools, their code is rarely seen.

This design can also be used for nonvisual objects, for core logic components of application frameworks. *Any* core logic components are also known as **business objects**, and their code is seen frequently.

Much More Java

The standard classes of Java version 1.2 were such a significant expansion of version 1.1 that it became commonly called "Java 2". Java 1.4 was another significant expansion, and Java 1.5 has some fundamental language enhancements. Because all of the versions since 1.2 have been "Java 2", it's a little confusing, so Java 1.5 is now known as "Java 2 version 5". The Java 2 classes are even separated into multiple *editions*.

- Desktop applications are most directly handled by Java 2 Platform, *Standard* Edition (J2SE), which is the edition most closely related to Java 1.1's functional scope.

- Network applications are addressed by the very well-known Java 2 Platform, *Enterprise* Edition (J2EE), which incorporated, and expanded on, extension packages to Java 1.1—most notably, `javax.servlet`. J2EE contains all of the J2SE packages.

- Handheld devices—like a cell phone and a Personal Data Assistant (PDA)—have limited memory capacities and therefore require small (**thin**) client software. Java 2 Platform, *Micro* Edition (J2ME) was created as a functional subset of J2EE, for thin clients.

Standardized Distributed Objects

Distributed Core Objects

To facilitate applications that have core pieces on multiple computers, to allow them to easily identify an object's location, J2EE came to allow creation of standardized distributed objects by adopting the JavaBeans with (completely different) *extensive* protocols, in a more complex configuration. These are **Enterprise JavaBeans** (**EJB**), and they're components of another container: an EJB container.

As opposed to one type of JavaBean, there are three types of EJBs: Entity Beans, Session Beans, and Message Beans. Each EJB type is tailored to a specific type of object; as opposed to just following a protocol, each of these must also extend a specific class. And the protocols require several types of pieces of code in each EJB type.

An EJB container requires a logically shallow type of configuration file called a **descriptor file**. For an EJB container, each definition is an **application deployment descriptor**.

Among other things, the protocols and the EJB container collectively create various types of objects for various aspects of network processing, create a pointer (**proxy**) to each object, and use the pointer as though it were the object. It's easy to see that an EJB container is another controller extension. And it's fairly easy to see that this functions as *a database for distributed business objects*.

The EJB design is a database for distributed objects, but it makes its stored entities *drive* the database management.

If it weren't designed for just Java, the EJB configuration would be even more complex. There's a design for components of any language that demonstrates this; it's the **Common Object Request Broker Architecture** (**CORBA**), and its container is the **Object Request Broker** (**ORB**). As much complexity and overhead as the EJB design entails, the ORB design requires more.

The EJB configuration itself becomes so complex because it puts *control of* the controller functions *in* the controlled entities. As just one effect, this immediately causes the need to *multiply* efforts, explicitly matching each subject process with a class. It has the same effect as making each of the stored entities of a database *drive* the database *management*; this approach is obviously fundamentally backward.

With comfortable understanding of the history of designs, a pattern can be seen here. Protocols can be shifted to the run-time system, or an extension, allowing developers to focus much more on their applications. And an extensible container allows extra developer control when it's needed. An example of this simplified design is the Spring framework. Compared with EJB, this process shifting is called **Inversion of Control** (**IoC**), but it's really just more-normal control.

This is a large-scale example of the fact that effective designing is all about understanding the best places to combine processes and the best places to separate them.

Server Processing Reorganization

Separating the presentation and core tiers of variable preprocessing works toward once again allowing pages to be developed by just authors and artists, with the functionality behind them being developed by programmers. This fairly independent development configuration can be accomplished by adapting aspects of the XML design (and the Ant design).

The Foundation

For fundamental consistency with traditional page development, servlet logic that generates HTML must be codeable in document form. With a particular arrangement of tags, and with an additional preprocessor (container), the HTML elements can be separated from elements that are translated into servlet code. All of it actually generates a servlet, and then some of that servlet writes the specified HTML, but the servlet code is in the document, in scripting fashion (similar to that on the client side), and HTML is in normal form. (It's fairly easy to see that this is a *fifth*-generation process.)

This is the original format of J2EE's **JavaServer Pages** (**JSP**). JSP has the servlet scripting elements (**scriptlets**) in a commentlike tag pair: `<%` and `%>`. It also enables a document attribute to reference a servlet data item value, with a different starting tag: `<%=` (but the same ending tag). JSP also has its own XML-style tags, which it calls **action elements**, oriented to straightforward handling of page-level tasks; for example, `<jsp:forward page="path">` forwards processing to another document. And, from the view of JSP, HTML elements are **template text**.

Before this occurs, with another usage of XML, JSP can direct processing for each type of request. This is handled through the `javax.servlet` package, with selective implementation of the `Filter` interface, based on the text patterns in the URLs, and one of the `Listener` interfaces, based on container-managed events, and creation of servlets for tasks other than HTML generation. Not only is this organized for link clicks, but the indirection of the `Filter` handles the fact that users can also enter URLs.

Also, *core* logic in JavaBeans, referenced with one of the `<jsp:useBean id="reference" ...>` tags, allows the JSP processor to manage page variables.

So, this is an overall design to smoothly serve each piece of an MVC configuration for dynamic content. URL requests to servlets are the controller. Presentation responses from JSP tags are the view. And core logic in JavaBeans is the model.

JSP version 1.0 was simply a management tool for HTML pages.

Building on Management

To tailor the added power of servlets to authors, JSP 1.1 enabled separation of servlet code and extended its management view by having that code in particular classes that create custom tags. Loosely based on Ant task customization, JSP custom tags are backed by a **tag handler**, by implementing one of the `Tag` interfaces or extending one of the `TagSupport` classes (which implement one of the `Tag` interfaces), from the `javax.servlet.jsp.tagext` package.

There are also **document directives**, which affect that whole document's JSP tag translations. Some of these connect a **tag library** (**TL**), through a descriptor file, with a **tag library descriptor**.

But, because servlets and then JSP 1.0 had been coded by programmers, and because creating custom tags is overkill for very simple code, programmers continued to frequently put scriptlets in documents.

To facilitate usage of tags, version 1.2 brought the JSP Standard Tag Library (STL), which put very simple code into standardized tags. The STL actually categorizes its tags by separating them into multiple tag libraries. The document directives associate each library with an abbreviation, which XML calls a **namespace**. By convention, the STL namespaces are constant; for example, `c` is for core actions, `fn` is for string functions, and `sql` is for database management.

The core library is oriented to the baseline programming level. Two of the most commonly used core tags are `<c:if test="code">` and `<c:forEach items="collection">`. There are also multilevel tag groups; for example, `<c:choose>` exists to contain `<c:when test="code">` and `<c:otherwise>` tags.

There are third-party software packages that support the JSP design. One is a framework that separates page navigation, for focused and flexible management of it; this is **Struts**. It allows navigation through Struts classes and an XML configuration file. Another is a tag library that enables document templates and plug-ins (for a cascading effect); this tool is **Tiles**. For example, `<tiles:insert attribute="name">` marks a point to allow a document to be inserted, and `<tiles:put name="name" value="document">` inserts one. Also, `<tiles:insert page="document">` plugs in a document at that point.

Refinement

JSP is about organization, so it's about flowing thinking. JSP version 1 allows referencing site variables in tags, but this is not in the same flow as the rest of tag syntax, because it requires a Java assignment scripting element, which also must have control of the entire value. JSP 2.0 adds implicit expression language (EL) for variable references; this allows a straight reference of the variable name, simply enclosed in braces, preceded by a dollar sign. Instead of `<tag att='<%= "text " + item %>'/>`, including the need for apostrophes (often called single quotes), EL enables `<tag att="text ${item}"/>`. So, JSP 2.0 has *complete consistency of syntax*. And it has *implicit variables*, which are assigned by the processor.

Also, elimination of the need for scripting enables just the `SimpleTag` interface and the `SimpleTagSupport` class to more smoothly serve the vast majority of custom tag definitions. Compared to what is now known as the "classic" tag handler scheme, these fewer classes each also have fewer functions needing customization.

Further, JSP 2.0 allows custom tags to be defined by authors, with other tags in a separate **tag file**. It's easy to see that this scheme is similar to the Tiles design.

Visual Object Implementation in a New Context

The basic JSP design goes a long way toward organization, but it's still a long way from the thorough organization of the object-oriented GUI design. The GUI design includes separated processing for each component and other separated processing for groups (collections) of components; each process includes component state and pointers to associated objects in the MVC design.

The complete tag-centric JSP 2.0 design points out that custom tags can create a similar organization by employing some indirection, associating each component (or group) with an object (JavaBean) and its corresponding property. This is taken further by allowing separate validator, observer, and renderer classes; these are referenced at the beginning of the response, instead of a servlet. This is the design of the tag library set JavaServer Faces (JSF) and the `javax.faces` package.

JSF's conventionalized namespaces are `h`, for HTML component-oriented tags, and `f`, for core GUI action-oriented tags. Two examples are the `<h:selectManyCheckbox>` tag and the `<f:selectItem>` tag, which sets the `h` tag's corresponding components; each of these tags has multiple optional attributes.

The JSF TL was obviously created from a very different point of view from the STL, which has procedure-oriented tags. One result is that mixing them in the same document is fundamentally inappropriate. JSF also *underscores* that pieces of procedural code—in any form—are best not mixed into documents, because that serves just immediate convenience and not the big picture.

To integrate request management functionality, JSF has its own EL processing. Instead of a dollar sign, JSF EL syntax uses a number sign preceding the left brace. Because they are processed differently, using JSF EL in the same document as JSP EL can become confusing.

As opposed to the procedure-oriented STL, the JSF TL is object oriented.

In achieving object-oriented organization, the JSF design is limited only by the network site configuration. As compared to the GUI configuration, it's necessarily more complex—comparatively *over*separated, requiring another layer. Site processing is inherently on (at least) two different computers, and the component processing is *not* on the presentation computer, so corresponding interactions cannot be as immediate. And state is not built into site components, so it must be maintained on its own.

JSF is a thorough management tool for HTML *components*.

The Variety of Syntax

Besides the progression of processing flows that have been addressed explicitly, this history implicitly demonstrates how a variety of syntaxes have been brought together to serve the combination of needs of progressing technologies. A prominent example is that programming languages are used in combination with tag languages, some of which reference expression languages.

Examples of one syntax being translated into another have also been explicitly addressed. For one, visual objects are translated into directives, as events; for another, expression language is translated into tag values, and tags are translated into Java. All of this also implicitly demonstrates that there are many ways to express the same processes. (In fact, the various programming languages described in Chapter One demonstrate the same thing.) Further, this demonstrates that the *best* ways have changed over time; they've accommodated differing mental flows, which have become more and more consistent.

The open nature of the industry's evolution—especially including concurrent creation of highly compatible technologies that were created for very different reasons—builds extensive complexities. Finally, this history implicitly demonstrates that more-consistently oriented syntaxes simplify development. Thoroughly consistent sets of syntax fundamentally help to keep the accumulation of technologies as simple as possible. The chapters of Part II each address this explicitly.

P A R T I I

Derived Simplicity

The second part describes in detail two examples of technologies that have emerged from consistent feeling for the spectrum.

■ ■ ■

x = Why
Interaction Algebra for Analyzing and Designing

This chapter delineates the syntax and application of interaction algebra for both function set networks and databases.

Function Set Network Representation

The most extensive usage of interaction algebra is for function set interactions. Designers who are already very familiar with each of the common function set interaction mechanism types (design patterns) will be able to very quickly get the feel of interaction algebra.

Syntax

The notations are extensive, but they're very straightforward. A *single* function set equation contains the same information as *multiple* UML diagram types.

The notations also have some flexibility. There is more than one way to describe some processes.

Expressions

Organization of Expressions

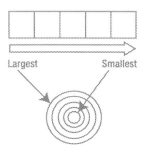

Largest   Smallest

Each function set entity is denoted by an expression that *represents entities in order from largest to smallest*; within an expression, a smaller entity is called a **subentity**. The syntax adheres to a pattern of $L_l C_c O_o F_f I_i$, where uppercase letters represent the *type* of entity and lowercase letters identify the exact entity.

Italicized uppercase letters are replaced by uppercase letters.

- C represents a type of class (P for parent, C for child, or S for single).

- O represents an object.

- F represents a function.

- I represents an item.

Italicized lowercase letters are replaced by numbers or dummy variables (which represent *any* occurrences).

- l is the particular lineage.

- c is the first (or only) child involved.

- o is the object.

- f is the particular function.

- i is the particular item.

Instead of a direct family, C can also directly represent interface functionality (X for interface or M for implementation). This is useful when classes can be just abstract and concrete, with *some* interface functionality, but it's required when they must be interface-only and implementation-included. For languages that do not explicitly accommodate interfaces, implementing the applicable interface functionality can be by just protocol.

Expression Example In words, each expression is usually simpler to describe from right to left.

- $L_2C_1O_oF_3I_2$ means the second item of the third function of multiple objects of the first child of the second lineage.

Of course, O_o, F_f, and I_i—an object, a function, and an item—each might be inappropriate for a given expression, and c is appropriate for only children. The combination of O_o and F_f or I_i denotes an object member. Also, F_f and I_i are often mutually exclusive, because the combination denotes a function-scoped item.

An O_o is required only when an object is *required*. No O_o indicates that an object is optional. When a function or item *must be* a class member, it is indicated with an exclamation mark in place of the O_o.

Distant ancestry is not a factor in interaction mechanisms, so there is no need for a C of G (grandparent), for example. And for S, family position is not a factor at all; in other words, it doesn't matter if a single has a parent or children.

Equations

Equation Left Side

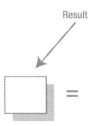

Result

Additionally, this syntax can appear before an =, denoting a result—a return or an outside effect—of a function. Multiple results can be separated by commas. Also, an × means that there can be any one of multiple results, and a 0 (zero) means that there is no return or outside effect.

Equation Right Side

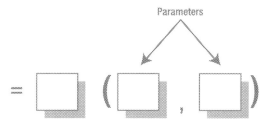

After the $=$, each expression must parenthesize another expression, because it must describe the function's parameters. (While parentheses are not the clearest representation of *code* parameters, they are the closest *mathematical* representation.) In place of an I, O specifically means no parameter, and U means a User (human user) specification; I_i means *any parameters*, which also means that no parameter is *required*. Layered parentheses denote the return of one call being the parameter of the next, and $+$ denotes a triggered call (from inside of a function).

Chronology

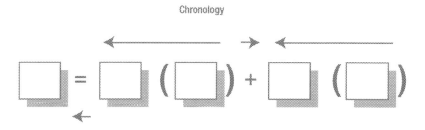

Chronological order is right to left in each parenthetical expression and around $=$s, and left to right among $+$s and through an equation set. Each equation must begin with at least one item, which can be a O, because any mechanism does.

Equation Examples A function set equation is often very densely packed, describing complex activity in a very short equation. Typically, an O or I expression, or both, is on the left side of the $=$, and a multilayered parenthetical expression, or multiple expressions, is on the right side. There are many common combinations.

- $L_1SO_1, L_0SI_1 = L_1CF_1(O)$ describes that an object is created, and a user item is set, by a child's function that has no input.

- $O = L_2PF_2(L_1PF_2(L_0SI_1))$ describes that nothing is returned, and there is no outside effect, from a function of the parent of one structure, which has input from the parent of another structure, which has input from the user structure.

Expressing Core Concepts

- Inheritance is simply reflected in a $C_c F_f$, because C_c inherits F_f from its parent.

- Static composition is (even more simply) indicated by any I_i.

- Dynamic composition is denoted by any $F_f(O_o)$, which shows that a function parameterizes an object.

- But aggregation, which is more of a *storage* mechanism than an interaction mechanism, is not simply expressed; its foundation is a set of $F_f(O_o)$ expressions.

- And dependence is $L_l C_c F_f(L_l C_c I_i)$.

Table 4-1 summarizes these expressions.

Table 4-1. *Core Concepts in Implementation Algebra*

Concept	Implementation
Inheritance	$C_c F_f$
Composition, static	I_i
Composition, dynamic	$F_f(O_o)$
Aggregation	Set of $F_f(O_o)$
Dependence	$L_l C_c F_f(L_l C_c I_i)$

Subscripts

By convention,

- Each subscripted number type is simply applied chronologically, starting at 1 and incremented by 1.

- For F with a dummy variable, corresponding parameters use the same variable.

- The lineage number starts at 0, which designates the user of the mechanism, and is incremented by 1. (In this context, the human user can be *thought of* as -1.)

- A lineage number on the left of the = indicates the user of the particular call, and an I with a dummy variable on the right of the = can indicate a *set* of items (i.e., the parameters of the corresponding function).

By convention, lineage 0 designates the user of the mechanism. All other entity types start at 1.

Equation Sets

Overall Syntax Organization

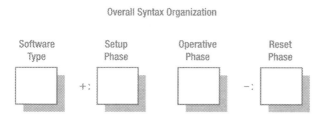

| Software Type | | Setup Phase | | Operative Phase | | Reset Phase |

Often, a mechanism requires a setup, and sometimes it also requires a reset. These are denoted by a prefix of +: and -:, respectively. The phases, including the main phase, are separated with a ^.

Between equations in a set of equations, ; denotes a succession of processes ("and"), and ? denotes differing processes of the same mechanism ("or").

A family structure can support multiple occurrences of the same mechanism. Each equation set describes *one occurrence*.

Each equation set describes a single occurrence of each mechanism.

Identification Notation

Each mechanism is identified with either a name—primarily for a mechanism *type*—or the mechanism's reference number within a system, followed by a colon and a description of the purpose of the mechanism. This identification is over the equation set.

Finally, a mechanism can be designed for a particular type of software. The software type precedes the purpose description, enclosed in parentheses. A means application, F means framework, T means toolkit, and S means system.

Shorthand

Shorthand can easily be thought of as a notation of the full notation.

L_i can be simply i (standard script), unless there are no other letters in the expression; for example, $L_i 0$ cannot be $i0$. For i, 0 may be omitted. For C, when there is a subentity, S and P may be omitted. And a constructor does not require an F. For each subscript—c, o, f, and i—when there is no corresponding 2 described, 1 may be omitted. (It should be remembered that even a single C implies multiple children.) And the A software type notation may be omitted.

Shorthand Examples

- I is shorthand for $L_0C\,I_1$, which is L_0SI_1.

- $1O$ expands to L_1SO_1.

- $3CF_2$ is $L_3C_1F_2$.

- C implies L_0C_1.

Of particular note, $ICOI_0$ specifically means a self-pointer. And IO on the right side of the $=$ means an object (and the location thereof) that is created by the caller; there is no need to describe the set-up phase for this. Also, an I on the left side of the $=$ defaults to the location of a created object.

Also, one mechanism can incorporate another, in any of its phases. Instead of duplicating the notation for the other mechanism, it can just refer that mechanism by its identification, with any specific entities each noted as a simple equation. The list of substitutions follows the reference in parentheses, separated by commas, with no spaces; for example, Factory($IS=2C$).

Name Notation

With interaction algebra itself simply conveying both structure and sequence, entity names can be indicated under the equation set, for more functional clarity, in a name equation: ICF_f = name. S is required here when it is implied in the equation set. O is required only when multiple objects of the same class are involved in a single occurrence of the mechanism. And the functionality of dummy-numbered entities is usually obvious enough to not require a name.

The name equations are best listed in order of *execution*. The name format is simply class.function or class.item. And the names can be general (functional) or specific.

Shorthand

A parent and a child can be named together, with parent/child.function.

When more than one entity in the same class must be named, only the first requires the lineage name or names; the rest can simply begin with the slash or period.

Context

Obviously, a description of each involved function is also necessary for complete understanding of any mechanism. This can follow the name: ICF_f = name: description. Even without that, though, the equation set for each mechanism type is unique.

Common Examples

As was mentioned in Chapter Two, across all of the function-oriented systems that have ever existed, all of the countless interaction mechanisms have been observed to be of just a relatively few types. All of the interaction mechanisms of any particular type have common characteristics (components and behaviors).

The following examples are interaction algebra representations of the most commonly identified function set interaction mechanism types. They are arranged, basically, from the simplest to the most complex. This serves to teach interaction algebra in a progressive way, but it also facilitates teaching the mechanism types themselves. (The book *Design Patterns* also mentions variations on these mechanism types. The examples can serve as *anchors* for the variations.)

Additionally, every equation identifies the user's connection point to the mechanism, which *Design Patterns* often excludes from its (free-form) diagram.

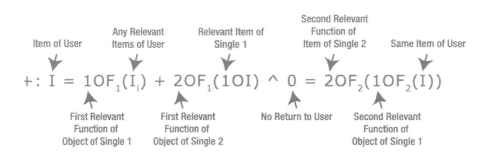

UML Structure and Sequence Diagrams for Labeled Example

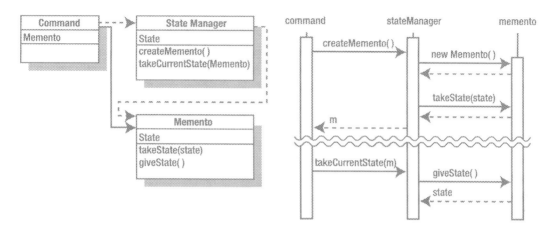

Strategy: To separate implementations from an interface, making the implementations dynamic

x = 1COF(I$_i$))

    1CF = ProcessType/Process.processType

Of course, this is the interface/implementation functionality built into some languages.

Wrapper: To add functionality to an object without extending its class

+: I = 1CO(I$_i$)+2O(1I$_i$)   ^   x = 1COF$_f$(I$_f$)+2OF$_i$(1OI$_f$)

    1C = DecoratorType/Decorator

    2S = Original

Design Patterns primarily calls this Decorator.

Singleton: To limit a class to one instance

$$+: \quad 1O, I = 1!F(I_i) \quad \wedge \quad I = 1!F(I_i)$$

$$1SF = Singleton.instance$$

Template: To define a process skeleton

$$x = 1CF_1(I_i) + 1CF_2(1I_i)$$

$$1CF_1 = Template/Completion.functionManager$$

$$1CF_2 = .function$$

Memento: To create a snapshot of an object's state so that it can be restored

$$+: \quad I = 1OF_1(1_i) + 2OF_1(1OI) \quad \wedge \quad 0 = 2OF_2(1OF_2(I))$$

$$1SF_1 = StateManager.createMemento$$

$$1SI = .state$$

$$2SF_1 = Memento.takeState$$

$$1SF_2 = .takeCurrentState$$

$$2SF_2 = .giveState$$

Adapter: To enable incompatibly interfaced classes to interact

$$x = 2OF(1COF(I_i)) \quad ? \quad x = 1CF_2(1MF_1(I_i))$$

$$1CF = Direct/Indirect.direct$$

$$2SF = Original.original$$

$$1MF_1 = Direct.direct$$

$$1CF_2 = OriginalType/Original.original$$

Constructor: To vary other classes' instantiation through the creator's extensions

$$2CO, I = 1CF(U)$$

$$1CF = ObjectManagerType/ObjectManager.newObject$$

$$2C = ObjectType/Object$$

Design Patterns primarily calls this Factory.

Factory: To create one or more objects without explicitly referenced classes

$$1O, I = 2OF_1(1CO(I_i))$$

$$1C = FactoryType/Factory$$

$$2SF = ObjectManager.newObjects$$

Design Patterns primarily calls this Abstract Factory.

Observer: To allow multiple objects' functions to be triggered when one object changes

$+: \ 0 = 1COF_1(I) \quad \wedge \quad L_1 0 = 1COF_2(1COI) \quad \wedge \quad -: \ 0 = 1COF_3(I)$

$1CF_1 = SubjectType/Subject.attach$

$1CI = .action$

$1CF_2 = .notification$

$1CF_3 = .detach$

Mediator: To manage the interactions of objects, allowing them to be more generic

$+: \ 1COI_i = 1COF_1(I_i) + 1O(1COI_0) \quad \wedge \quad x = 1CF_2(OI_0) + 1CF_f(1COI_f)$

$1CF_1 = MediatorType/Mediator.newColleagues$

$1CF_2 = .colleagueFunction$

Bridge: To make a logical parent-children relationship allow each to change independently

$+: \ Factory(IS=2C) \quad \wedge \quad x = 1CF_f(I_f) + 1PF_g(1CI_g) + 2CF_h(1I_h)$

$1C = Abstraction/RefinedAbstraction$

$2C = ImplementationType/Implementation$

Composite: To treat individual objects and compositions of them in the same way

$+: \ I = 1C_2OF(1C_1OI_0) \quad \wedge \quad x = 1C_1OF_f(I_f) \quad ? \quad x = 1C_2OF_f(I_f)$

$1C_1 = Component/Individual$

$1C_2F = /Composite.addIndividual$

Builder: To independently manage the construction of a multilevel composition

$+: \ I = 2O(1CO) \quad \wedge \quad 0 = 2OF_1(I_i) + 1COF_f(2OI_f)$

$1C = BuilderType/Builder$

$2SF_1 = BuilderManager.build$

Command: (T) to isolate a call in an object, allowing dynamic function sets

$+: I_1, I_2 = 2CO(1O(I_i)); 0 = 3OF(I_2) \quad \wedge \quad 0 = 2COF_f(3I_f)+1F_f(2I_f)$

$1S$ = Receiver

$2C$ = CommandType/Command

$3SF$ = Invoker.addCommand

Chain: (S) to create a succession of handlers of types of directives

$+: I_3 = 1C_cO(I_1, I_2) \quad \wedge \quad x = 1C_cF(I_4)$

I_1 = topicType

I_2 = nextHandler

$1C_cF$ = HandlerType/Handler.handle

I_4 = topic

Flyweight: To enable large-scale sharing of sets of objects

$+: 2CO_o, I_2 = 1F(I_1) \quad \wedge \quad x = 2CF_f(I_3)$

I_1 = key

$1SF$ = FlyweightManager.newFlyweight

$2C$ = FlyweightType/Flyweight

I_3 = externalState

State: To establish dynamic sets of functionality based on state

$+: 1OI_1, I = 1O(I_i); \quad \text{Singleton}(L_1=2C)$

$\wedge \quad 1OI_2 = 2CF_f(1OI_0); \quad x = 1OF_f(2CI_f)$

$1SI_1$ = Owner.state1

$2C$ = StateFunctionType/StateFunction

$1SI_2$ = .state2

Proxy: To encapsulate complex access to an object

$+: I = 1C_1O(I_i)+\text{Singleton}(L_1=1C_2) \quad \wedge \quad x = 1C_1OF_f(I_i)+1C_2OF_f(I_f)$

$1C_1$ = Subject/Proxy

$1C_2$ = /Actual

Iterator: To provide generic traversing services for a collection of objects

$+$: $I_1, I_2 = 2CO(1O(I_i))$ $\wedge$ $x = 2COF_f(I_f) + 1COF_g(2COI_g)$

  $1S = $ Collection

  $2C = $ IteratorType/Iterator

Prototype: (F) to create one or more objects through cloning

$+$: $I_1 = 2CO(1C_cO_1(I_i))$ $\wedge$ $1C_cO_2, I_2 = 1C_cO_1F(2COF_f(I_f))$

  $1CO_1 = $ PrototypeType/Prototype.original

  $1CF = $ .clone

  $2CF = $ FactoryType/Factory.newObject

  $1CO_2 = $ .clone

Visitor: To organize functionality across a family by the functions

$+$: $I_1 = 1CO(I_i);$ $I_2 = 2CO(I_i)$ $\wedge$ $x = 1COF(I_2) + 2COF(1OI_0)$

  $1CF = $ ElementType/Element.acceptVisitor

  $2CF = $ VisitorType/Visitor.function

Facade: To centralize and simplify access to a subsystem

$+$: $x = 1O(I_i) + lO(1I_i)$ $\wedge$ $x = 1OF_f(I_f) + lOF_f(1OI_f)$

  $1S = $ Facade

Resulting General Observations

Function set network interaction algebra serves as a thorough notation for function set interaction mechanisms, *to concisely communicate and clarify function relationships* and to help to identify, complete, and describe any new mechanism types. Interactions are at the level of interfaces; in this pure abstraction, the *f(x)* notation is appropriate for parameters.

Interaction algebra evidences that interaction mechanisms are, most clearly, techniques for manipulating, and thus maintaining, design variables. Ultimately, function orientation gets its frequently mentioned "elegance" from its algebraic properties; very simply, techniques for manipulating variables are elegant.

Database Representation

Database representation has a much simpler syntax than function set network representation, but it has the same format *structure*.

As Chapter Two explained, as the designing of an actual system unfolds, just as classes can be seen to simply define complex (compound) data types and how they are processed, class designing can be seen to simply be the *databasing of functions*. There are many similarities between class designing and standard database designing; there's a common feel, especially for relational databases, because they dynamically link tables, with one having the parameters for another. (This view is reinforced by the capability of embedded SQL, with which tables also store the code for common functions.) Basically, in both types of designing, the combinations of similarities and differences define how entities can be shared. But, again, function orientation has added complexity; function databasing can be seen as an inheritance of standard databasing, with more factors to balance. Sharing needs determine whether all of the items of a set should go into one table or a group (a team) of tables—item subsets. And, as in any type of designing, there are always balances of consideration of space versus time; an extension of this, for function orientation, is the consideration of static versus dynamic entities.

And at interaction algebra's level of structure, more similarities between class designing and standard database designing become evident, and more understanding of *each* arises.

Syntax

Each database entity is denoted by a syntax that has a tTI_i pattern, where italicized uppercase letters are replaced by uppercase letters and italicized lowercase letters are replaced by numbers. t is the particular table, T represents a type of table (T for base table and E for extraction), and I represents an item; i is the particular item. Of course, I_i might be inappropriate for a given expression.

Additionally, this syntax can appear before an =, denoting a result of an operation. Multiple results can be separated by commas.

After the =, an expression can parenthesize another expression, to describe the selection parameters. 0 means no parameter, and U means User (human user) specification. Layered parentheses denote the return of one selection being the parameter of the next, and + denotes a compound selection. Chronologically, each equation must begin with an item, because any mechanism does. Between a set of equations, ; denotes a succession of selections ("and"), and ? denotes differing versions of the same selection ("or").

By convention, the subscripted number is simply applied in chronological order—which is right to left in each parenthetical expression and around =s, and left to right among +s and through an equation set—starting at 1 and incremented by 1. Corresponding subentities should use the same number (or dummy variable). And, by convention, the extraction number starts at 0, which designates a User query, and the table number starts at 1; both are incremented by 1.

Equation Examples Contrary to that of a function set network, a database equation is often very simple but very lengthy. Typically, an E expression is on the left side of the $=$, and several T expressions are on the right side; this is a "select" operation. An update has a T expression on the left side.

- $1E = 1TI_1 + 1TI_2$ describes an extraction of two items of a table.

- $0E = 2TI_2(1TI_1)$ describes a User query of one item from one table that is selected with one item from another table.

Sometimes, a mechanism requires a setup, and sometimes it also requires a reset. These are denoted by a prefix of $+:$ and $-:$, respectively.

Shorthand

For t and i, when there is no corresponding 2, 1 may be omitted. (But a t of 0 must appear when a User query is involved.)

Shorthand Examples

- $0EI$ is shorthand for $0EI_1$.

- E expands to $1E$.

- TI implies $1TI_1$.

Resulting General Observations

From the function-oriented point of view, stored data is an object, and the map for that data is a class. A table is a persistent object, and an extraction is nonpersistent. There is no inheritance from one table to another (though the ramifications of the concept are very interesting), and a "join" operation is multiple inheritance from tables into an extraction.

Interaction Algebra II

The format of interaction algebra is its key. The specific characters of the syntax are not fundamentally important; this, of course, is another property of algebra. In fact, with the format understood, the further level of description can be accomplished by following any A_a with the name of the entity, probably enclosed in brackets. *This enables a seamless transition to programming.*

```
+:  1[parent-name] O[object-name], I[item-name]
      = 1[class-name] !F₁[function-name] (0)
```

Also, use cases can be represented with constants as parameters. As with standard algebra, plugging in constants identifies more characteristics of a particular usage of a structure. With interaction algebra, the flow of a particular use case can be identified.

As teams of designers become familiar with interaction algebra, mentally translating to corresponding diagrams becomes easier. Their generic flow makes this second nature. At that point, it's easy to see drawn-out diagrams as training wheels.

Interaction algebra is only in its infancy. As it matures, it is believed that the thorough notation will be able to be *manipulated* with specific algebraic methods. This would serve to ensure that a mechanism is in its simplest form (in other words, optimized), and it could reveal many more (specifically focused) characteristics of any mechanism.

Further, nongraphical data and process representations are more fully compatible with the type of *live* analysis that is a very frequent part of development.

From Chapter Two, perhaps the most far-reaching ability of interaction algebra is how it might be able to thoroughly clarify *combinations* of mechanisms, as an integral part of a whole-system design. Just as in standard algebra, the objective is to maintain the algebraic characteristics—manipulating variables, not inserting constants; of course, in both, this type of effort can be cumbersome, but (in both) its often necessary.

The simplifying and combining features of interaction algebra can be used together to address whole-system optimization. This is a broad version of refactoring, which easily relates to algebra; they both have "factors" and "factoring" processes.

For identification of all of the properties and possibilities of interaction algebra, widespread experimentation and discussion are highly recommended.

■ ■ ■

CHAPTER FIVE

Live and Unscripted
Object Animation, a Clearer View of Automation

This chapter delineates the philosophies behind data-oriented designing and, further, demonstrates utilization of a different *type* of software language to completely support it. This type of language is also more closely expressive of the development process. Further, it integrates features of another concept called **aspect orientation** (which allows even-more-independent functionality), in a more controlled way than other aspect-oriented approaches.

As just a detail language, for low-level designing, this type of language provides a *seam-less* transition from designing to programming and can be very directly translated to any other language. But as an actual programming language, with automated translators (pre-compilers) to other languages, it provides the most far-reaching benefits, maximizing the ability to design on demand. (And maintenance on existing systems benefits from reverse translators.) The syntax section is also an open specification for that.

More Data Orientation

It's fundamentally important to see that, as opposed to a procedure-oriented *list of com-mands*, a data-oriented account is a *sequential description*. This is a huge shift in mind-set. It's also fundamentally important to see that a data-oriented step-by-step account of a function does not leave out any information. It's all there; it's just from a different point of view.

It's fundamentally important to see that a data-oriented chronological description does not leave out any information. It's all there; it's just from a different point of view.

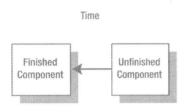

The most straightforward view of a data-oriented program is that it's a description of products and, more directly, their components *through periods of time*. This view eliminates the competition between data and processes, in effect, placing processes as a *derivative* of data. Actually, in the data-oriented view, a program is a **product set**, and its functions are **interval**s. So, in the data-oriented view, function orientation is **interval orientation**.

The idea of data orientation is arrived at from another direction as well, providing further confirmation of its validity. After a high volume of instances of figuring out the processes that are involved in accomplishing tasks, the processes become more and more second nature and, therefore, require less and less thought. The thoughts that remain significant are those that are focused on the products of the tasks.

The benefits of data orientation are very strong. Interval orientation adds a dimension to it. With the common focus on object state, it can be seen that, with each step, an object changes. So, *each interval is a sequence of states of objects*. This definition is similar to that of animation. Data orientation, therefore, demonstrates clearly that automation is most effectively seen as *object animation*.

Automation is most effectively seen as *object animation*.

A fundamental philosophical anchor is found in the comparison of application-oriented software to function-oriented software in the context of data orientation. Reviewing procedure orientation, an application-oriented program is a structure subset, and a class is a function set; these are, of course, views of software from *two differing directions*. In data orientation, an application-oriented program is a product set, and a class is an **interval set** (or **set**); *because an interval is derived from a product, in data orientation, both views of software are from the same direction*. Thinking this further, in data orientation, an application-oriented program is, more accurately, a product *phase* set (because multiple programs do different things to the same data), and a class is a product set. So, an interval set *is* a product set; *this is self-evidence that data orientation is the natural orientation of classes*.

In data orientation, a structured program is a product *phase* set, and a class is both an interval set and a product set. This is self-evidence that data orientation is the natural orientation of classes.

And a fundamental philosophical anchor related to the design is found in the fleshing out of interval-oriented entities.

- A state is a set of values; it's zero-dimensional.

- An interval is a sequence of externally seeded variables, and that's one-dimensional.

- A class is a set of intervals, which is two-dimensional.

- And an object, which is a class with internal variables, is a full three-dimensional entity.

Data Relationship Management

The key observation that unlocked the possibility of data-oriented languages is that procedure-oriented languages boil down to operations that copy data from one place to another, compare data from different places, perform math, and control operation list sequence. Beyond that are just *variations in combinations of these operations*. Therefore, the operational range of languages is so straightforward that *a language doesn't need verbs.*

The operational range of languages is so straightforward that *a language doesn't need verbs.*

Without verbs, the procedure orientation is gone. The language is fundamentally simplified, and the developers are freed to be able to think about the results, the products, the purposes. Then, data relationship management serves, and is served by, a reorientation in interval naming conventions, changing what the names answer from hows to whats.

Without verbs, the procedure orientation is gone.

In general, and inside of interval sets, structured logic best serves understanding of the purposes (the whys—the combinations of whats) of a system, which serves maintenance and redesigns. So, ultimately (especially for code clarity in common business environments), structured logic shouldn't be just facilitated by a language; it should be made unavoidable. And the concept should be carried even farther than is traditional, in multiple ways.

First of all, observation of common purposes shows that the copying of data from a file (a "read"-type command) is frequently the source of control of operation list sequence. So, this copying is more important than any other operation, and sequence control is well served by giving it dedicated syntax.

Second, observation of common programming efforts, especially in maintenance, shows that nested condition structures ("if"-type commands) easily become needlessly complex and an annoyance to navigate. More philosophically, nested condition structures are not a user's notion, and they draw focus away from the products; in fact, this is probably why they're needlessly complex. They should be strongly discouraged; branching should be encouraged. All scopes should be named, while retaining and still conveying the scope hierarchy. And, actually, this facilitates identifying the condition with a name, which, once again, serves understanding of the purposes.

Likewise, code values often convey no meaning. They should be discouraged, except in definitions (of named data items, which convey meaning).

Lastly, object creation solely for the purpose of an interval call in the same step (chaining) is two-dimensional logic, and this should be clearly reflected visually. This requires a revolutionary concept: a visually two-dimensional statement. The exact technique for this turns out to be very simple. Its syntax is delineated later.

In short, "dream" languages serve clear thought and simple design. The business-type languages are rigid because they are too oriented toward the user in their functionality. The C-type languages, while very flexible, are cryptic because they are too oriented toward the computer in their syntax; they were designed by engineers, for engineers. DRM languages are so straightforward simply because they leverage user-oriented syntax and a view that easily orients the user to management of tasks. DRM languages are so clear that comments and separate documentation are usually counterproductive (because of the added efforts needed to keep them coordinated with the code). Probably the only reason for comments is to describe a multilayered entity. Taking the concept to the limit, with a fully compiled (or semicompiled) DRM language, the compiler orients the *computer* to management of tasks. Then, reverse translators serve as transitional tools.

Direct Effects on Programming

With a data relationship management language, the direct effects on programming are fundamental and dramatic. Again, there is a revolution in philosophy.

With a DRM language, programming is simply *organizing components*, rather than figuring out procedures, all the way down to each character.

In essence, software development is *teaching* a computer a system, especially as the developers are learning it.

A DRM language is, then, a low-level designing tool that *replaces* programming. (It's almost cheating.)

A DRM language maximizes the ability to let the compiler in on the design.

A Dream Language

The first DRM language was created in 1993. Originally called Goal-Oriented Language of Development (GOLD), it grew out of observation of a system that had become severely convoluted over time, with needlessly complex logic. It was further observed that the reason for this complication was a general lack of focus on the purposes of the system.

The lack of focus translated to a breakdown between high-level designing and programming. In fact, the low-level design was being significantly impacted by the code, and even the mid-level design was beginning to be impacted. In other words, the programming was driving the designing; this of course, was backward.

The fact that programming could go so far astray pointed to a need for more overall control of that effort. It pointed to a need for better flow from design to code. It pointed out the two directions of thinking and the resulting bottleneck. The most effective answer revealed itself to be an extension to designing—with a new type of language.

The idea of specifying value sources for output fields was merged with the columnar format of report layout generators and, more directly, assembly languages. This went back beyond the verb mnemonics of the assembly languages, functionally reinterpreting computer (machine) code. In effect, in some ways this was a new *second*-generation language.

Data relationship management (and the "dream" pronunciation of DRM) replaced the name GOLD, because it's a more-detailed description of what this kind of language entails.

Later, it was determined that, because the languages simply established relationships between components, another format, built on *labels*, was also possible. In this scheme, as opposed to fitting *between* command keywords, each type of entity is *identified*; in other words, the keywords describe exactly what the entities *are*, instead of how they are used. This concept is easier for programming novices, because its elements are extremely obvious. Although the label-driven language was developed independently of tag (markup) languages—like HTML and, more versatilely, XML—their proliferation is ample evidence of the viability of the concept. Because of the completely descriptive nature of this DRM language, and also because DRM languages are unlike the standard fourth-generation procedure-oriented logic mechanism, scripts, the name "Descript" (de·script') was given to this format.

The original format, then effectively a shorthand for Descript, was named "D". It is still more efficient for programming veterans, and, unlike Descript, it's a very visual language, based on clause organization, so it's very appropriate for interval orientation. Of course, D is a reasonable name because there's a language named C. D and Descript can be seen as *dialects* of the same language. Actually, it's easy for a compiler to translate D to Descript; in fact, this is a good diagnostic tool. Therefore, it's also possible to utilize a flexible combination of the two.

The combination, with added features of abbreviations, is actually a third dialect, and it makes the label concept more practical. It was named "Desc", because it's halfway between D and Descript, and because it's pronounced like "desk", which reflects its very comfortable fit for business situations.

The vocabulary and punctuation of all of these dialects are specifically designed to make standard software operations very obvious. They are not committed to, and therefore limited by, the syntax of any other languages—except for human languages. They are simply committed to the mental angle of development. In fact, DRM languages, by themselves, clarify the development process.

Syntax of D

This section describes the D dialect. The least complicated way to present this syntax is to cover its (priority) data-oriented features first and then its (derivative) interval-oriented features; this is what's done in this section. As an indication of the simplicity of this type of language, note that, as short as this section is, it isn't an *overview* of the syntax; it's basically the entire syntax. Throughout the presentation, the reorientation to procedure of each of the features is covered, using C-type (mostly Java) vocabulary. Regarding D as just a low-level designing language, implicit steps described indicate added steps that a programmer includes in code.

Everything about a product set is logically derived from **product**s. Each product set is logically in a **product line** (or **line**) of related basic functionality; this is defined simply by the product set definition file's folder structure under a folder named "Product Lines". In procedure-oriented languages, a product line reorients to a package. A **package** is a basically self-sufficient logical grouping of product lines; it reorients to a library. For some perspective, a package is, in nontechnical (mostly marketing) vocabulary, a product.

The **major entities** of a product set are the **characteristics set** and the interval. Each of the major entities defines the scope of **minor entities**. A characteristics set can define either **permanent** or **temporary** characteristics (entities). Basically, the characteristics that are defined as permanent can be shared directly with other product sets; those that are defined as temporary can be shared directly between intervals.

The minor entities are as follows. A **part** is, roughly, any most practical subset of a product or resource. It reorients to a record. A **component** is any smallest practical piece of a product, resource, or product set. It reorients to a data item. Larger pieces are a **component group** (or **group**), which reorients to a structure; and a **component series** (or **series**), which reorients to an array. A group or a series is also a component.

Each of the major entities is defined by a collection of **statement**s—a **header statement** and **body statement**s. Header statements reorient to interface declarations (signatures), and body statements reorient to data declarations and commands, depending on the context. Before all of these can be **set statement**s, each of which describes a **set property**, which is a basic set definition, documentation, or a shortcut.

For context, it's helpful to understand that nearly every body statement is a logical **step definition**, which simply describes a **step**; a step is simply a logical step of progression through a process. Step definitions are specifically baseline, nonorganizational descriptions, and there are very few functionally blocking body statements.

A **managed interval** has one or more **management component**s, which reorient to parameters. (Sometimes, a management component is a *subject* of the interval; other times, it's a controller.)

A **jump** is a change of sequence from within one interval to the beginning of another, through that one and back to the point that follows the beginning of the jump; it reorients to a call. (A recursive jump is allowed to only managed intervals.)

Intervals never fall through as they are listed, from one to the next; the end of an interval implies a return. The end of the main interval implies a return to the next-higher-level product set. The top-level set returns to the operating system.

General Formats

First of all, spaces can be embedded in entity names. In other words, normal titles can be used, instead of awkwardly compressed ones.

```
End of Resource
```

is possible, as opposed to

```
endOfResource
```

Also, entity names can have double hyphens. And they can have single hyphens, provided that those are not *preceded* by spaces; in other words, no word can begin with a hyphen. No other punctuation is recommended in entity names.

```
User-specified Shape
```

is valid, as is

```
Marked Group -- End Column
```

With the accommodation of embedded spaces, some keywords are actually **keyphrase**s; a keyword is also generically a keyphrase. All of the (very few) keyphrases are lowercase, to allow all of the entity names to be easily differentiated with title case. Further, punctuation can be used *in place* of any of the main keyphrases; they cannot both be used, because that is redundant. Except for enclosers and semicolons, punctuation should be separated from entity names by spaces.

Every line in a product set is a descriptive *statement*. There are up to three **column**s in each statement, to serve generic functionality: the **component column**, the **source column**, and the **control column**. These are *variable width*, separated by vertical slashes: │. All *trailing* vertical slashes are optional. (As for the computer's point of view, *execution is right to left*. This is essentially how the reorientation occurs.)

The organization of **component definition**s, which reorient to data declarations, is basically traditional, because data declarations have already been data oriented; they don't have verbs. But they could have; this is another indication of the viability of non-verb step definition (body) statements, as is the syntax of assignment commands in most languages.

```
take 1, make it smallint, name it x
```

is not necessary in any language.

```
copy 1 to x
```

is not necessary in most languages.

An entity **reference** reorients to a data name or a message. (Just for clarity at this point, an interval-oriented aspect of D needs to be mentioned. A **locater** reorients to a reference. It is used exactly like any other component, except its value can't be set explicitly. A locater is for an object only and is *most simply thought of as the object itself.* There is no component type that reorients to a pointer.)

Because the whole concept of DRM languages is that they are simply sequential descriptions, all statements begin left justified. An indentation indicates **continuation** of the previous line. It is recommended that two spaces be used, for visual clarity.

Likewise, entity names should adhere to the following convention: there should be no verbs in interval names; the name should describe what the interval *is*, not what it *does*. A sound approach to this is to name the interval the same as the result of the process when that is simply a component—for example, "Area" or "Location". When the main purpose of the interval is a process, it's best to give the interval the *name* of the process—for example, "Validation" or "Extraction", or even "Hold" or "Hide" (which, in this context, are nouns)—sometimes appended to the name of a subject component. When a result component can be arrived at by more than one method, the interval name can be the component followed by "by" and the process name. (It's interesting to note that this context frames the accurate usage of the word "method".) Other times, it's appropriate to give the interval the name of a situation—"Empty Layout" or "Data Error". Because of the entrenched history of often—but not always—using verbs in names, these conventions can sometimes require an effort to orient to, but the consistent mentality they result in is always worth it.

A good indication of the small amount of analytical effort a DRM language requires beyond common, nontechnical levels is the fact that the common-title names of closely related entities can vary by modifier words that the names contain, but the *modifier words should be immediately before the correct subject words.*

```
Keyed Report Line
```

technically says that the entire report is keyed, whereas

```
Report Keyed Line
```

technically says that just the line is keyed.

A **comment** is denoted by a statement starting with an asterisk: `*`. Again, the need for this should be rare with a DRM language. When it is needed, it should *follow* the statement it clarifies.

```
* In normal writing, an asterisk indicates a note following its subject.
```

NAME TRANSLATIONS

Concerning translation to other languages, any entity name is implicitly the D entity name with the spaces removed and the first character made lowercase (except for classes). Also, access and update interval names implicitly translate to method names with a get or put prefix, respectively.

Further, the **alias table** can be established (outside of any product set), in a file named "alias table", to implicitly translate any other noun-based interval name to a corresponding verb-based method name. Each entry is simply the **alias** interval name enclosed in angle brackets, followed by the translation. This table must be populated explicitly.

Set Definitions

Another product line can be referenced implicitly, specified with a statement that must come at the beginning of the product set. This is a **line implicit reference**; it begins with a line reference, followed by one or more set names, separated by commas. For clarity, every applicable referenced set should be specified. This reorients to an import statement (or an include directive in C++), and multiple sets reorient to an asterisk. A line reference has the line name enclosed in braces; line hierarchy levels are separated by colons.

```
{D : Math} Circle
```

Each **product part completion** (or **completion**), which reorients to a write, or **resource part access** (or **access**), which reorients to a read, can implicitly reference an interval. This allows references to that interval to stand out, as a completion or an access. Any **part implicit reference** statement must come after any line implicit statements. In the first column is, optionally, the completion interval name enclosed in angle brackets: `<` and `>`; in the second column is the store name and the part name, separated by a colon, enclosed in brackets: `[` and `]`; and in the third column is, optionally, the access interval name enclosed in angle brackets.

```
<Keyed Report Line Product> | [Keyed Report : Keyed Report Line]
   | <Keyed Report Line Resource>
```

An alias may be applied to just within the product set, with an entry outside of the alias table, after any part implicit statements. This statement has the alias interval name enclosed in angle brackets, followed by the translation.

```
<Option Selection> selectOption
```

Fundamental Body Statement

It's best to explain one type of body statement at this point, because it can be integrated into some header statements.

Component Definitions

A component definition has the component name followed by brackets in the first column. A **component type** (or **type**), which reorients to a data type, is optionally between the brackets. Component types are the same as any C-type data types. An initial value is optionally in the second column. The keywords `null` and `false` can also be a backslash: `\`; the keyword `true` can be a double backslash. No specified type indicates the smallest possible appropriate type; *no specified value indicates an appropriate zero (initialization)*. Neither specified indicates a null string; this is used for stack placement.

```
Response []
```

is equivalent to

```
Response [string] | null
```

Major Definitions (Header Statements)

There can be at most one **permanent characteristics definition**, indicated by a statement that is a double hyphen, followed by the keyword `permanent`. This can be followed by another double hyphen. Any component definitions that are in this definition reorient to static (class) data items. This must come after all implicit definitions.

```
-- permanent --
```

is equivalent to

```
-- permanent
```

And there can be at most one **temporary characteristics definition**, indicated by the keyword `temporary` between the double hyphens. Any component definitions that are in this definition reorient to instance data items. This must come after the permanent definition.

An **interval definition** is denoted by a header statement that has the interval name enclosed in angle brackets. This is followed by the interval's **return component definition**, which should be on its own line, to make both the interval and its return obvious. The return component's type is enclosed in brackets in the first column, and an initial value can be in the second column. By default, *the return component's name is the same as the interval name*; a different name can be specified. If there is no return component, then the brackets are empty.

```
<Picture Validation>
  Picture Valid [bool] | false
```

For a managed interval, the **managed interval definition** includes a **management component definition** list, with component definitions, each preceded by a colon: `:`. In each definition, the optional value is a default value.

```
<Picture Validation : Width [int] | : Height [int] |>
  [int]
```

When the sole purpose of an interval is to produce its return component, that *type of interval* is a **function interval**. It is denoted by the left angle bracket preceded by the keyword `function` or a question mark without a space following it. This makes the purpose of the interval very obvious.

```
function <Picture Valid>
  [bool] | false
```

    is equivalent to

```
?<Picture Valid>
  [bool] | false
```

A component that is defined in an interval definition is an **interval component**, which reorients to a method data item. This is the most common component scope. Likewise, a component that is defined outside of an interval (temporary or permanent) is a **noninterval component**.

There is a special feature that functionally promotes interval components, for clarity and convenience. This is specifically to allow using a referenced interval to create components *for* the referencing interval. It's extension of an interval, for organization, and it is, effectively, a referencing interval inheriting from a referenced interval. This is an **extension interval**. The left angle bracket is preceded by the keyword `extension` or an exclamation mark with no space.

```
extension <Context Acquisition>
  []
```

    is equivalent to

```
!<Context Acquisition>
  []
```

Within the interval, any statement that causes the interval to not be self-contained—in other words, any statement that affects something in a parallel logic structure—should be marked as a **side effect**. This is simply a *self-contained* standard comment that doesn't affect the statement at all; it just makes the statement stand out visually, denoted with a slash as the first character. So, the slash *is* the comment. *These are not allowed in a function interval.*

```
/ active body statement
```

Minor Definitions (Body Statements)

The first (component) column can contain a component definition; a component reference, which here reorients to a receiving item; or a product part reference, which indicates a completion.

The second, or source, column can have a component reference (or an explicit value), which reorients, here, to a copied item; a **combination**, which reorients to a calculation; or an **interval reference**, which reorients to a message.

The third column—the control column—can contain a **control incrementation**. This can be a specialized component incrementation or interval reference, or it can be a resource part reference, which indicates an access. Regardless of these, the third column can contain a **sequence modification**: a **specific usage**, which reorients to an if; or a **repetition**, which reorients to a while; or both—which function as a selective grouping.

When either (or both) of the first two columns has something, and the third does also, this is a **compound statement**. So, part of a compound statement controls the rest of it.

More Component Definitions

A component **group definition** has the component group name and the left bracket. This is followed by the **group member** component definitions, followed by a statement with just the right bracket, all of which can be indented. The philosophy here is that the member components are the group's type. No member component name indicates that it is a **group alignment member.** (In nonblock procedural languages, an alignment member reorients to filler.) A group must contain more than one member. One group can be defined within another, to unlimited levels. Because of the allowed indentations here, any multiline member definition must use a semicolon as a **continuation mark**.

```
Keyed Report Line [
    Sequence Number [smallint] | 1
    [smallint]
    Department Number [smallint]
    ]
```

A component series is an extension of a group; it's a group that has all members of the same type, assigned a position number. A component **series definition** follows the group definition format, but the series name is optional, and an optional size name and a size value, separated by a vertical slash, enclosed in angle brackets, precede the left (square) bracket. The size name cannot be referenced; it exists just to serve identification of the purpose of the size. The first position in a series is indexed as 1 (not 0), for clarity; the size must be greater than 1. The optional value is copied to each occurrence of the **series member**. One series can be defined within another, to unlimited levels.

```
Report Page Spacing <Lines Per Page | 60> [Character Count [smallint] | 2]
```

and

```
<Estimated Maximum Employees | 100> [Employee Number [int]]
```

Also, series can be defined within a group, and groups can be defined within a series. Similarly, a series *can* contain more than one member. Further, either can be used as a type, effectively copying its structure, in any subsequent component, group, or series definition.

String definitions can be more specific than those for null strings, of course. These other definitions require the length to be specified. The simplest specification indicates that the length is equal to the length of the value. This is the same as the null string format, except the value is in place of the null keyword. Otherwise, the definition follows the series format; except, here, simply "string" (or nothing) is between the brackets, and the optional value clause is outside of the brackets. For clarity, the string type is translated to a series of "character" members, defined as the type "char", because the component is really *a string of characters*.

```
Status Message <Characters Per Line | 132> [] |
   "Products were completed without incident."
```

translates to

```
Status Message <132> [character [char]] |
   "Products were completed without incident."
```

It is highly recommended that *symbolic values* not be used in step definitions. They each should reside in a **constant component**, which must be defined. This forces purpose to be as clear as possible. There are also standard constant components (for example, January [smallint] | 1).

```
Print Control | Double Spaced Line |
```

instead of

```
Print Control | "0" |
```

Component References

Any component reference can list multiple components, separated by commas (specifically not colons, because those occur *between* component references). This is a **component list** (or **list**), and it's good for components that can be grouped obviously—for example, coordinates.

```
Coordinates
```

can be

```
Last X, Last Y
```

It also allows a **multicomponent return**, which can be copied to either a group or a list. (This special feature is accomplished with an extra implicit step that creates and uses an interval group.) The **return multicomponent definition** must include names, and its individual return components are separated by commas.

```
?<Target Location : Width [int] | : Height [int] |>
  X [int] | 0, Y [int] | 0
```

A unique group member can be referenced by just its name. Any nonunique member must be referenced in a **group member reference**, which is the member name preceded by each of its owner levels' name until one of those is unique. This reference must begin with the keyword group or an at sign: @; the levels must be separated by colons, and all of it must be enclosed in angle brackets.

```
<group Original Report Line : Print Control : Another Component>
```

is equivalent to

```
<@ Original Report Line : Print Control : Another Component>
```

A **series member reference** must begin with the keyword series or a number sign: #, followed by all of its series level indices' name, separated by commas; then a colon; and then the member name. No specified series levels indicate all of the occurrences of the member; this is useful when the series is unnamed.

```
<series Week Number, Employee Counter : Hours Worked>
```

is equivalent to

```
<# Week Number, Employee Counter : Hours Worked>
```

and

```
<series : Hours Worked>
```

is equivalent to

```
<# : Hours Worked>
```

When a series is in a group, or vice versa, a reference to a low-enough member requires a mixture of syntax. The series label is needed anytime the level type switches to series. The group label is needed only for the highest level of the reference. This is possible because the colons already indicate that that entity is a group. In a string reference, the character member is implied.

```
<@ Response : # Character Number>
```

references an individual character.

Combinations

Source combinations are the same as C-type operations, with a few exceptions.

A plus sign or minus sign without a component name following it implies an addition or subtraction, respectively, of *1*. When the resulting component is the same as the first component of the combination, that component is in the first column and the rest of the combination is in the second. (For a standard component incrementation, these two shortcuts are combined; just the plus sign or minus sign is in the second column.)

```
Group Mark Column | Group End Column +
```

and

```
Group Begin Column | + Group Mark Column
```

and

```
Column Counter | +
```

Also, the operation sign for a string concatenation is an ampersand: &. But this is not required between a literal and a reference, in either order. It is required only between two references.

```
Result Message | "The next valid transaction "
   "number is " Transaction Main Number & Transaction Check Digits
```

To facilitate constant components, there are two types of strings that are implicitly updated each time they are referenced. The first is an **incomplete string**, which reorients to a tokenized string. In an **incomplete string definition**, for each place of string insertion, it has simply a set of angle brackets with *nothing* between them. Then, an **incomplete string reference** is a component list of the string name and the insertion string components, in order.

```
Availability Message [] | "The room is available on <>, from <> to <>."
```

The other type of implicitly updated string is a special feature: a **dynamic string**. It has implicit construction when it's referenced, because there's a standard string construction in the **dynamic string definition** itself. It's simply denoted by a single set of angle brackets just before the first part of the string. The advantage of a dynamic string is that it has a normal component reference; it doesn't require a component list.

```
Availability Message [] | <> "The room is available on " Target Date
  ", from " Start Time " to " End Time "."
```

Product Part References

A product part completion has beginning and ending markers—left and right brackets—to allow explicit grouping of product part processing. The grouping form separates the right bracket into its own statement; it is recommended that completion be handled in this manner whenever possible. In its simpler form, a completion can be the product name enclosed in brackets.

```
[Report Keyed Line
* all of the components populated
]
```

   and

```
* components populated in various places
[Report Keyed Line]
```

A product part completion can describe special handling with an appended keyword. removal and replacement can also be a left angle bracket (a less-than sign) and both angle brackets together (a less-than-and-greater-than sign), respectively. These reorient to a delete and a rewrite, respectively. Actually, normal handling can optionally be described with addition or a right angle bracket (a greater-than sign).

```
[Report Keyed Line removal ||]
```

   is equivalent to

```
[Report Keyed Line <]
```

   and

```
[Report Keyed Line replacement
```

   is equivalent to

```
[Report Keyed Line <> |
```

and

```
[Report Keyed Line addition |
```

is equivalent to

```
[Report Keyed Line > ||
```

A shared part must be preceded by a colon, preceded by the desired product.

```
[Sorted Report : Report Line removal]
```

Interval References

A jump is triggered by an interval reference and is delineated by the interval name being enclosed in angle brackets, in the second column. Function intervals and extension intervals are referenced with their respective keyword or punctuation preceding the left angle bracket, just as in the definition.

```
| <Attribute Check>
```

and

```
Pixel Count | ?<Picture Size>
```

A **managed interval reference** has two formats: one short and one long. In the short format, the interval name is followed by the management component values or other component names, each preceded by a colon.

```
Goal Number [] | ?<Random Number : 1 : 100 : 0>
```

Even though it's more effort, the long format is highly recommended because, with it, each interval's purpose is more obvious, which makes it much simpler to learn how to use all of the intervals. Further, it allows more flexibility, with multiple purposes for the same component type. This format has each colon preceded, *with no space*, by the management component name; this combination is a **label**. Because of the occasional consecutive entity names (which can embed spaces) here, each management component name must be preceded by a semicolon.

```
Goal Number [] |
   ?<Random Number; Low Number: 1; High Number: 100; Decimal Places: 0>
```

A PEEK AT DESCRIPT

The syntax between the angle brackets in the long managed interval reference follows the same format as the Descript dialect.

Interval reference **nesting** is very clearly identified by where the angle brackets of the nested interval reference are.

```
Component Value | ?<string segment : Report Layout
  : Column Counter : ?<string length : Original Value>>
```

Even more clarity regarding execution sequence is possible with a two-dimensional statement. For the nested portion, in place of the component is a caret: ^. For the interval reference portion, in place of the nested interval reference is another caret. This special feature simply resembles a text editing insertion.

```
^ | ?<string length : Original Value>
Component Value | ?<string segment : Report Layout
  : Column Counter : ^>
```

There is no syntax for nested component copies, including from a combination or to a definition (even with an implied copy), because these make sequence complex—because they are not data oriented.

Specific Usages

A specific usage is described with an appended sequence control, in the third column. for, which basically reorients to "if", followed by a condition, can also be parentheses surrounding the condition.

```
| <Header Skip> | for Print Control = Page Break
```

is equivalent to

```
| <Header Skip> | (Print Control = Page Break)
```

This next feature is mildly tricky, because of what people are very accustomed to with the "if" orientation. Because of the for orientation, the condition controls and and with reorient to "or" and "and", respectively; they can also be a comma and an underscore, respectively. As with the reorientations, with takes precedence over and; parentheses are also used for grouping. (Bit-level and and with simply require bit-level component definitions.)

```
| <Group Code Process : Group Type> |
  for Group Fields
   with (Column Counter = Group Begin Column
   and Column Counter = Group End Column +)
```

is equivalent to

```
| <Group Code Process : Group Type> |
(Group Fields
  _ (Column Counter = Group Begin Column, Column Counter = Group End Column +))
```

THE AND-WITH MIND-SET

The mind-set for the condition controls is that what is being described is all of the conditions that that step applies to. This is in line with the focus on all of the possible components of the system (because this best serves identification of purpose).

The comparison operator is negated with a backslash preceding it with no space.

A normal specific usage statement can be immediately followed by a specific usage statement that specifies the opposite condition, with the keyword others or a not-equals. This reorients to an "else".

```
| <Layout Check : Symbol Count> | for others
```

is equivalent to

```
| <Layout Check : Symbol Count> | (\=)
```

One special feature, the keyphrase all opposite, signifies the reverse of every comparison of the previous corresponding and condition control clause; it can also be ><. Any lower-level (parenthesized) set of comparisons is treated simply as an others condition.

For

```
| <Group Code Process : Group Type> |
  for Group Begin Column > Low End Range
  with Group End Column < High End Range
  with (Column Counter = Group Begin Column
    and Column Counter = Group End Column +)

| <Default Process> |
  for all opposite
```

is equivalent to

```
| <Default Process> | (><)
```

and translates to

```
| <Default Process> |
 for Group Begin Column \> Low End Range
 with Group End Column \< High End Range
 with \(Column Counter = Group Begin Column
  and Column Counter = Group End Column +)
```

Another special feature is designing-stage **transitional code**: beginning a statement, the keyword or, which can also be a question mark, signifies that a design decision has not been made. It's a double comment, of the two statements that it separates, and it is provided to facilitate concise working notes in the code. This is how the or condition control fits into the consistent mind-set; during compilation, it generates a warning.

```
Line Position | +
or Line Position | + Field Length
```

is equivalent to

```
Line Position | +
? Line Position | + Field Length
```

A **parallel specific usage** (or **parallel**), which reorients to a switch, is designated by each of the involved statements starting with a hyphen.

```
-  | <Main Line Process> | for Special Attribute = Main Line Attribute
-  | <Redefine Process> | for Special Attribute = Redefine Attribute
-  | <Table Process> | for others
```

Repetitions

A repetition is described with the sequence control for every followed by a condition, which can also be braces: { and } surrounding the condition. This is most often implemented in conjunction with a control incrementation, creating an **incrementation set**, which can exist regardless of whether the other columns have anything in them.

Resource Part References

A resource part access is just the name of the resource (or resource part) in the third column.
   A shared part must be preceded by a colon and then the desired resource.

```
|| Original Report : Report Line
```

Incrementation Sets

The order of the control column clauses is for, for every, and control incrementation. Again, they are executed from right to left. But the starting point can be either before or after the incrementation; in other words, the incrementation can be executed either first or last. Incrementation first is the default. Incrementation last is denoted with the keyword `last` or a left angle bracket preceding the incrementation notation. Incrementation first can be specified with the keyword `first` or a right angle bracket preceding the incrementation notation; alternately, it can be a left angle bracket *following* the incrementation notation, or nothing. If there is no keyphrase or punctuation between the incrementation notation and the previous clause, then that clause must end with a semicolon.

```
|| for every Print Control \= Double Space first Report Original Line
```

is equivalent to

```
|| {Print Control \= Double Space} Report Original Line
```

CONTEXT OF FOR EVERY

The `for every` sequence control is a good reminder that the context of body statements is sequence. It doesn't specify every time that the condition occurs in the entire product set; it specifies every time it occurs *consecutively*.

Instead of an access, the control incrementation can be just the incrementation component, followed by an arithmetic operator and an incrementation amount. Further, instead, this can be an interval reference; the interval cannot return a component. When the incrementation is arithmetic, the component is created and initialized implicitly (when necessary). The initialization must be done explicitly, in a preceding statement, for a nonzero initial value. This is in line with the fact that any variance from the simple incrementation set sequence must be done explicitly, for maximum clarity.

```
|| {Column Counter \> Line Width} Column Counter + 1
```

Functionally, the incrementation set reorients to the `for` configuration, in a controlled way, because it doesn't allow just any statement as the incrementation or (one-time) initialization. It also can increment the first time through, for simplicity, because that can sometimes be the functional initialization.

Specific Blocks

Because products are the primary focus, and conditions are secondary, no visual blocking is allowed. Specific usages and incrementations *can* have immediate **follow-up steps**, which reorient to a block; each **follow-up step definition** starts with a plus sign. *Appropriately*, it's obvious that this feature cannot be used for multilevel logical structures; for these, interval references must be used.

```
[Source Code || (Source Code = Not Written)
+ Source Code | Empty Layout Message |
+ ]
```

Status Management

Status monitoring is on-and-off (functional block) based and has two forms: single statement monitoring and multiple statement monitoring. Multiple monitors can occur together, and they can be turned off in any order. The single form must be the monitor statement (or statements) immediately preceding the statement that is being monitored. And the multiple form must be a monitor-on statement before the monitored statements and a monitor-off statement after; *a return implies an off.*

The multiple form starts with a left brace for an on or a right brace for an off, and the single form starts with both braces. Both forms have a `for` clause that can be applied to an implied "status" component and an implied status value component name; in these statements, `status =` is optional. This syntax is actually specialized, shortening `for <# status count : status name> = "Status Name"`; the "status name" series and "status count" component are implicitly defined.

```
{} Unexpected End of Resource || for status = End of Resource
```

is a single,

```
{ Unexpected End of Resource || (End of Resource)
```

is on, and

```
} || (End of Resource)
```

is off.

Implicitly, each status name is added to the series, and the status count is incremented; status processing references them in reverse order (functionally, as a stack). Any developer-defined status name, type (information, warning, error, or severe), and description can be explicitly maintained in the **status table**, in a file named "status table", and referenced at any time. After successful status processing, execution resumes at the statement following the monitored statements. All of this reorients to a try-catch-finally functionality, with multiple areas of less overhead.

Miscellaneous Statements

An explicit return from an interval is denoted by the keyword return or a period in the first column and, optionally, a component name or value in the second.

```
return | 0 |
```

is equivalent to

```
. | 0
```

Specifically for translation to structured languages, a product set is referenced with the set name enclosed in brackets and nothing as the interval name.

```
| <[set-name] : args>
```

A direct return to the referencing product set is designated by the keyphrase set return or a double period.

```
set return | status |
```

is equivalent to

```
.. | status
```

A product or resource **start** reorients to a file open, and a **finish** reorients to a file close. They are denoted by the part or resource, followed by the keyword start or finish, in the first column and nothing in the second column. Typically, these are not stated explicitly; their necessity is handled in standard status intervals. A **restart**, which reorients to a close then an open and has the same format as the other two, is appropriate for getting the part pointer set back to the beginning; this must be stated explicitly. Typically, it's the only one of the three that is used.

```
Original Report restart ||
```

is equivalent to

```
Original Report finish
Original Report start
```

To help to ensure complete compatibility, another language's **idiom** is designated to remain intact with a backslash in the first column. As usual, indentation continues this to multiple lines. Effectively, this is a comment that gets its comment character stripped. Of course, then, the language must match the one that is being translated to.

Interval Orientation

There is only one class per interval (product) set, and it *is* the name of the interval set; the name of the class isn't actually *in* the interval set. The first statement (after implicit-reference statements) is the **ancestry statement**, which is the full ancestry of the class, in reverse order, with a greater-than sign at the beginning and preceding each successive ancestor. This is for both definition and documentation. The original ancestor of every class is the "generic" class; it is never specified.

```
> Shape > View
```

An **interface-only class** has just the keyphrase `interface only` as the first statement; this reorients to an interface. An implementation of an interface-only has the **implementation statement** following the ancestry statement; this has a double greater-than sign at the beginning, followed by one or more interface-only class names, separated by commas.

```
>> Error, Message
```

An **interface-only interval**, which reorients to an abstract method, has just the `interface only` keyphrase in its body. A class that has any, but not all, interface-only intervals is an **incomplete class**, which reorients to an abstract class. It has just the keyword `incomplete` as its second statement.

```
> Shape > View
incomplete
```

An **object definition** has the object name enclosed in parentheses, followed by the class name enclosed in brackets, in the first column. A **generalized object**—an object defined as one type and initialized as a specialization of that type—is denoted by an ancestor, enclosed in brackets, between the two other entities. In the second column is the keyword `initialization` as an interval reference. The `initialization` keyword designates the object creation (in the heap) and a reference to the initialization interval of the class specified in the first column. Any class must have at least one initialization interval, any of which must explicitly indicate a return component type that is the same as the class. Within that interval, the copying of the object's location to that component is *implied*.

```
(User Shape) [Shape] [Circle] | <initialization : Radius>
```

In common function orientation, it's possible to implement an execution-time type-specific collection, with reflection for each member and designation of the type during collection initialization, from reflection of the first member. For a compile-time version, C++ has templates; these add another layer of complexity to that language. Instead, there is a non-modifiable **specializable type**, which creates an object whose exact type is not determined until usage—somewhat the opposite of a generalized object. It is denoted with the ancestor name enclosed in parentheses inside of the brackets; this can be of any specificity, all the way down to generic. The class is implicitly specified by the class of the first object that is copied to the specializable-type object.

```
(User Shape) [(Shape)] | <initialization : Radius>
```

An **object** (locater) **reference** has the object name enclosed in parentheses. If the overall reference is to an entity of the object, then the object reference is before the entity name. A **class reference** has the class name enclosed in brackets, before the entity name. An explicit **line reference** has the line name enclosed in braces before the class name. For intervals, all of these are within the interval reference. In short, this is a visual representation of the layering, as opposed to a stringing.

```
Radius | ?<(Focus Circle) Radius>
```

and

```
Area | ?<[{D : Math} Circle] Area : Radius>
```

The keyword `parent` or a tilde, `~`, as the class denotes the parent class. The location of the object that the statement is in is denoted by the keyword `object` or an exclamation mark as the object. This reorients to the `this` keyword. With the `t` preword, it's rarely needed.

```
| <[parent] Rendering>
```

is equivalent to

```
| <[~] Rendering>
```

and

```
Old Length | (object) Length
```

is equivalent to

```
Old Length | (!) Length
```

A **type change**, which reorients to a cast, is denoted by a component reference in the first column and the new type, enclosed in brackets, preceding the source in the second column.

```
(Focus Shape) | [Circle] (Previous Shape)
```

Interaction Properties

Both components and intervals have interval set **interaction properties**, which define how any entity interacts with other entities. These are more loosely coupled than their reorientations.

The **usability** determines what types of entities can use the entity being defined, with any one of the keywords any, line, ascendants, or self following the component type or the return component definition. These reorient to public, no keyword, protected, and private. The default is self.

```
Pi [] any | 3.14159
```

and

```
?<Area : Radius [float]>
  [float] any
```

The **rigidity** determines when the entity being defined can be updated, with any one of the keywords definition, execution, or variable. This follows the usability specification, if it exists. Final (or static in C++) is reoriented from execution for a component and definition for an interval. An interval's rigidity cannot be variable, though its management components' can. And it should be kept in mind that a definition rigidity is very rarely appropriate. The default is execution.

```
Pi [] any execution | 3.14159
```

and

```
?<Area : Radius [float]>
  [float] any execution
```

A variable component's usability can be only self, so it is not specified. The component can be used by other interval sets with **access interval**s and **update interval**s, which reorient to accessor methods (getters and setters). These are interval names that match a noninterval component name, without or with parameters, respectively. (They are also interval names that match a noninterval collection name, with one parameter or multiple, respectively.)

Further, the standard (single statement) access and update intervals can be designated as an **implicit access** or **implicit update**, respectively, in the component definition, with the keywords out and in, respectively, separated by a comma, enclosed in parentheses, in place of the usability property.

```
Radius [float] (in, out) variable
```

and

```
Radius [float] (in) variable
```

and

```
Radius [float] (out) variable
```

and

```
Radius [float] () variable
```

A self interval that is referenced by a single interval can be designated, in the interval definition, to use the referencing interval's components directly; logically, this makes the interval a **block interval**—a block of the referencing interval. Its usability specification is replaced with the name of the referencing interval, enclosed in angle brackets; this also reflects more-specific usability than self. As context for a block interval, an extension interval can be referenced by multiple intervals.

```
?<Area>
  [float] <Shape Statistics> execution
```

An interval that has no return component and default interaction properties does not require a return component definition statement. [] self execution *is implicit.*

Interval definitions can come before the temporary characteristics definition; they are *part of* the characteristics sets. The **durability** is simply defined by which characteristics set the component or interval definition is in. And it is important to remember that *a permanent statement cannot reference any temporary characteristic (internally).*

There are a few values, in two categories, for a component name prefix that are highly recommended as a convention, because they make *less* frequent purposes more immediately obvious. This is a **component name pre***word* (or **preword**), because it's separated by a space. One of three values identify which type of definition the component is (directly) defined in—permanent, temporary, or management—with p, t, and m, respectively. One of three other values identify how the component is used—that it's a variable, dynamic string, or incomplete string—with v, d, and i, respectively. The two categories can be combined into one preword, with the definition identification first.

```
v Radius [float] (in, out) variable
```

    and

```
p Pi [] any execution | 3.14159
```

    and

```
tv Old Length [] self variable
```

    and

```
<Area : m Radius [float]>
```

Advanced Elements

Chaining is possible with the two-dimensional nesting statement. For the object creation portion, in place of the object name is a caret. For the interval reference portion, in place of the object creation is another caret. Again, this feature simply resembles a text editing insertion.

```
^ [Circle] | <initialization : Radius>
| <^ Rendering>
```

Reflection has two parts. First, any object has a "class" interval (provided by the generic class), which returns the name of the class of the object. Second, any string can be turned into a "reflection" object and examined. So, these can be combined.

```
User Class [string] | <(User Object) class>
Object Documentation [reflection] | User Class
```

> can be combined into

```
Object Documentation [reflection] | <(User Object) class>
```

Advanced Comparators

For clarity, locaters cannot be compared with the equal sign; they must be compared with either of two generic intervals: "same object as", which is implemented (in generic) with the equal sign, or "equivalent to", which is an empty interval, because it's different for each class (but it's not an interface-only interval, because it's not required to be implemented). For ease of use, these generic intervals can be referenced with standard keyphrase syntax.

```
Same Values Count | + | ((Current Object) = (Desired Object))
```

> is illegal.

```
Same Values Count | + | ((Current Object) equivalent to (Desired Object))
```

> is clear and is equivalent to

```
Same Values Count | + | (<(Current Object) equivalent to : (Desired Object)>)
```

> and

```
Same Object Count | + | ((Current Object) same object as (Desired Object))
```

> is equivalent to

```
Same Object Count | + | (<(Current Object) same object as : (Desired Object)>)
```

Using reflection are the generic intervals "type of", which compares an object to a class, and a special feature, "same type as", which compares two objects.

```
Same Values Count | + | ((Current Object) type of [Desired Class])
```

and

```
Same Object Count | + | ((Current Object) same type as (Desired Object))
```

Advanced Locaters

To accommodate Java, an inner class is defined with a header statement of the inner class name enclosed in double brackets. It is referenced internally with the inner class name enclosed in double brackets. Externally, the outer class name is between the double opening brackets. An anonymous inner class is not possible; this is another example of the restriction on visual blocking.

```
[[Mouse Monitor]]
```

and

```
[Inquiry Form [Mouse Monitor]]
```

More directly, a locater can contain an interval location. This *can* be called an **interval locater**. The location is copied with the standard interval reference enclosed in parentheses. An interval reference with an interval locater is the same as with an object locater, without a further interval name.

```
(Action Monitor) | (<Action Performed>)
```

and

```
| <(Action Monitor) : Action>
```

Aspect Orientation

Separate from interval (function) orientation and data orientation, the emerging concept of aspect orientation allows more independent development of the various aspects of a system, specifically separating (auxiliary) things like security and logging logic from the (core) business logic. In its emerging common form, it's done through post-compile code injection, "weaving" the aspects together, guided by flexible (wild-carded) string searches *by the auxiliary aspects*. Actually, aspect orientation can be seen to extend interval orientation in that it increases the interoperability between intervals.

While this does create an integrated result, it seems to have some fundamental problems. It's a brute-force method that puts auxiliary concerns in control of core concerns, eliminating important encapsulation. Further along this line, it requires either one class's detailed knowledge of other classes' implementations or all classes' adherence to a strict interval and component naming standard; otherwise, its string searches are ultimately limiting in their power, not allowing a high degree of intelligence in the substitutions.

These problems can be solved functionally by separating any logical interval into successive subintervals, promoting necessary interval-level components to temporary level, and allowing *any* referencing object, including an aspect, to inject its logic between subinterval references. This enables the core concerns to maintain control and makes the injection points as intelligent as possible, but it's also tedious and cumbersome.

A shorthand for this functionality is explicit **inlet**s into a (single) interval. The referenced interval has inlet names, each surrounded by double angle brackets, in the second column, to mark the inlets. And the reference doesn't have a right angle bracket; its statement is followed by **injection** definitions, any of which are ignored if its name doesn't match any of the inlet names. An injection begins with an injection header, which has the injection name enclosed in double angle brackets, and is followed by the statements to inject. Injections can't be syntactically nested. The injection definitions are followed by the interval reference's right angle bracket in a statement by itself.

```
<Server Interval>
* some core statements
| <<Security -- Login>>
* more core statements

<Client Interval>
| <(Server) Server Interval
<<Security -- Login>>
| <(Third-Party) User Validation>
>
```

With this device, the inlet names can be as general or specific as desired, independent of the implementations. The string searches are on the inlet names, so only these require a naming standard.

This actually serves as a reverse reference for the server interval, extending a longtime technique—passing a service object—to the interval level.

Injections can be in an interval outside of an interval reference, for all subsequent interval references within that interval; so, later definitions replace earlier ones. In this case, any noninjection code must be marked by a preceding statement that is just a (single) right angle bracket. And they can be before the interval definitions, for all interval references within that class.

Further, they can stand alone or in a group, in an **injection set**, denoted by a file name with a caret prefix. It is referred to (functionally copied), anywhere in a class or other injection set, with the injection set name, including the caret, enclosed in double angle brackets.

```
<<^ Security>>
```

To serve clearer purpose, one more fundamental integration of aspect orientation is that each class must ascend from an **aspect class**, which is denoted by the keyword aspect as the first statement, instead of an ancestry statement; the generic class is the only ancestor of an aspect class. The standard aspect classes are "language"; "Utility", "Mediation", and "Application"; and "View", "Model", "Security", "Logging", and "Persistence".

An Application-ascendant class is the starting point for direct execution by (human) users. In it, the "application" interval reorients to the main method. It must be a permanent characteristic with management components for the count of user-specified parameters and the parameters themselves, no return component, and an any usability. Application is the default ascendant class, and, in an application, the application interval is required.

```
-- permanent --
<application : parameter count [int] : parameters <> [string]>
  [] any
```

Reserved Words

To reiterate how few reserved words D has, the following is the list of all of its reserved words.

Keyphrases

Controls

and	for every	set return
equivalent to	return	with
for	same object as	

Modifiers

addition	group	removal
all opposite	incomplete	replacement
aspect	interface only	restart
extension	last	series
finish	or	start
first	others	

Properties

any	execution	self
ascendants	line	temporary
definition	permanent	variable

Values

false	null	parent
initialization	object	true

An Example of D

Although the D dialect has been applied to product sets that have hundreds of lines of code, the most appropriate example at this point is a fairly simple one. The best way to convey how straightforward D code is, is to put it next to the most popular extended procedure-oriented language, Java. Listings 5-1 and 5-2 demonstrate this comparison. Further, the best way to get across the fundamental advantage of a DRM language is to show the various stages of design, *as the product set in common language smoothly becomes the product set in DRM language.* This is done in Listings 5-3 through 5-6.

Listing 5-1. *The Guessing Game, in Java*

```
public class GuessingGame {
    public static void main(int argv, string args[]) {
        GuessingGame guessingGame = new GuessingGame
    }
    private GuessingGame() {
        string response = null;
        while (response = "y") {
            final smallint goalNumber = Math.random() % 100 + 1;
            smallint playerNumber = 0;
            sysout.println ("Guess my number.");
            smallint lowNumber = 1;
            smallint highNumber = 100;
            while (playerNumber != goalNumber) {
                sysout.println ("The number is from " + lowNumber
                        + " to " + highNumber + ".  Your guess:");
                playerNumber = sysin();
                if (playerNumber < goalNumber) {
                    sysout.println ("Higher.");
                    if (playerNumber !< lowNumber)
                        lowNumber = playerNumber+1;
                }
                if (playerNumber > goalNumber) {
                    sysout.println ("Lower.");
                    if (playerNumber !> highNumber)
                        highNumber = playerNumber-1;
                }
            }
            sysout.println ("Right.  Do you want to play again?");
            response = sysin();
        }
    }
}
```

Listing 5-2. *The Guessing Game, in D*

```
> Application

-- permanent --
<application : parameter count [int] : parameters <> [string]>
  [] any
(Guessing Game) [Guessing Game] | <initialization>

-- temporary --

<initialization>
  [Guessing Game]
Another Round | "y"
Response [string] variable
| <Round> | for every Response = Another Round

<Round>
Goal Number [smallint] | <[Number] Random Number : 1 : 100 : 0>
Player Number [] variable | 0
| <To Screen : "Guess my number.">
Low Number [] variable | 1
High Number [] variable | 100
| <Clue> | for every Player Number \= Goal Number
| <To Screen : "Right.  Do you want to play again?">
Response | <From Screen>

<Clue>
| <To Screen : "The number is from "
  Low Number " to " High Number ".  Your guess:">
Player Number | <From Screen>
| <To Screen : "Higher."> | for Player Number < Goal Number
+ Low Number | Player Number + | for Player Number \< Low Number
| <To Screen : "Lower."> | for Player Number > Goal Number
+ High Number | Player Number - | for Player Number \> High Number
```

Possible D Design Stages

Listing 5-3. *The Guessing Game, in D, Design Stage 1*

```
Goal Number | Random Number
Guess my number, from 1 to 100.
Higher.
Lower.
Right.
```

Listing 5-4. *The Guessing Game, in D, Design Stage 2*

```
Goal Number | Random Number
Guess my number
Low Number | 1
High Number | 100
The number is from Low Number to High Number.
Higher. for Player Number < Goal Number
+ Low Number | Player Number +  for Player Number \< Low Number
Lower. for Player Number > Goal Number
+ High Number | Player Number --  for Player Number \> High Number
Right. for Player Number = Goal Number
```

Listing 5-5. *The Guessing Game, in D, Design Stage 3*

```
Goal Number | Random Number
Guess my number.
Low Number | 1
High Number | 100
| <Clue> for every Player Number \= Goal Number
Right.

<Clue>
The number is from Low Number to High Number.
Higher. for Player Number < Goal Number
+ Low Number | Player Number +  for Player Number \< Low Number
Lower. for Player Number > Goal Number
+ High Number | Player Number -  for Player Number \> High Number
```

Listing 5-6. *The Guessing Game, in D, Design Stage 4*

```
Goal Number | Random Number
| To Screen : "Guess my number."
Low Number | 1
High Number | 100
| <Clue> | for every Player Number \= Goal Number
| To Screen : "Right."

<Clue>
| <To Screen : "The number is from " Low Number " to "
  High Number ".  Your guess:">
Player Number | <From Screen>
| <To Screen : "Higher."> | for Player Number < Goal Number
+ Low Number | Player Number + | for Player Number \< Low Number
| <To Screen : "Lower."> | for Player Number > Goal Number
+ High Number | Player Number - | for Player Number \> High Number
```

And the final design stage is, again, in Listing 5-2.

Conclusion

So, the current standard views of software objects are noticeably foggy—somewhat misleading, overly complex, and fundamentally incomplete—and, therefore, significantly counterproductive.

In their most complete form, objects (and classes), which are data oriented, have data-oriented code—in a data-oriented language. Data relationship management is the technique of, and the key to, data-oriented languages; they are then, more directly, DRM ("dream") languages. The effect of data orientation is a clear view of a system in its execution form, as a collection of successive data states; this is the clear view of object animation.

The clear view is of processes being derivatives of data—intervals of data states. It is of objects and classes being forms of interval sets and the network design being interval orientation, requiring interval-oriented features of DRM languages. The clear view can easily be seen as the *digitization* of processes, as opposed to the analog view of extended procedure-oriented languages. This simplification of mind-set will *propel* all forms of systems development.

Further, for ongoing development and redevelopment, because a DRM language always puts the result—the purpose—of any statement first, it's fundamentally easier to learn the functionality of any piece of code with a DRM language than with procedure-oriented languages.

Also, specifically, the organization of D makes it visually the code equivalent of drag and drop. It therefore gives the drag-and-drop concept the power to be applied to every bit of software. This actually allows the entire development process to be done with a drag-and-drop mentality, along with some of a fill-in-the-blanks mentality (for naming and text). And it allows tools to be built on that foundation.

There are very few actual development languages; there are more *variations* on these languages. Further, a language itself is just syntax; *behind* that is the processing that the language causes. This is another example of interface and implementation. What's commonly thought of as a language is, most accurately, a language *processor*. Even before DRM languages can be used for programming, they can be used for detailed designing—and documenting.

Because interval-oriented development has more objectives than does application-oriented development—being more geared to ongoing development—it is well served by more *areas* of documentation, but much less of each. This includes for each potential system variable that was identified but designed constant and for each interval set interaction mechanism. Interaction algebra is a very structured, very concise notation for analyzing interactions and designing mechanisms.

Addressing system efficiency, the design has more impact than the language. The most effective designing is served by understanding the *meaning* of interaction mechanisms and language features. And understanding is simplified with philosophical insight, which allows thinking up a level, such as that classes are compile-time states of a family, and an interval-oriented system is a network of sets of structured utilities—effectively, an interval database—that has a *virtual hierarchy* of functionality and is generated partly through decomposition.

Identification of the interval sets is strategically accomplished with a balance of the bidirectional considerations of the network, depending on the purpose of the *design*. Identification of the individual intervals is best served with a mentality that focuses on the set; for example, a set provides an item access (an "*item*", not a "get*item*") and an item update (a parameterized "*item*", not a "set*item*"). And interval set interactions must be well organized, because a poorly organized network actually makes changing it more complex.

Interval orientation is an investment in the future.

Reading Recommendations

With the fairly simple guidance of this overview established, one of two paths is recommended:

- Programmers are likely to find the most immediate benefits by studying the "Orientation"-related books, then the "Untangled Web", and, finally, the "Bi-design".

- Designers can most easily study the "Bi-design" and "Untangled Web" books. After *that* pursuit, the "Orientation" books (one language at a time) complete a full spectrum of understanding, for the ability to create the best designs.

Orientation

Programmers who are new to function-oriented languages can most easily read language "best practices" books, using language explanation books (especially the O'Reilly Press books, because of their organization and reasonable conciseness), first for just reference, then, separately, for deeper study.

For learning C++, it's clearest to learn Java first, then the added complexities of C++. In either language, there are other books that are best for just reference, because they are *extremely* long.

- For those who want to learn Java, *Hardcore Java* (O'Reilly, 2004), by Robert Simmons, Jr., is an excellent best-practices book that has a lot of functional insights. And *Learning Java, Second Edition* (O'Reilly, 2002), by Patrick Neimeyer and Jonathan Knudsen, is very comprehensive.

- For those who want to learn C++, *Effective C++, Second Edition* (Addison-Wesley, 1997), by Scott Meyers, is much like *Hardcore Java* for C++, but it's not as structured. And *Practical C++ Programming, Second Edition* (O'Reilly, 2003), by Steve Oualline, is an excellent explanation book. Occasionally, *Practical C Programming, Third Edition* (O'Reilly, 1997), also by Steve Oualline, is helpful in explaining even more fundamental features.

- Smalltalk books are difficult to find, but Objective C is explained, along with Apple's Cocoa development environment (the next generation of NeXTSTEP), in *Learning Cocoa with Objective-C* (O'Reilly, 2002), by James Duncan Davidson and Apple Computer, Inc. After reading all about C++ and Java, this book is an absolute breeze.

Bi-design

Exploration in designing should be geared to building a feeling for function, more than just a collection of knowledge; this serves the ability to manage the designing process. *Better, Faster, Lighter Java* (O'Reilly, 2004), by Bruce A. Tate and Justin Gehtland, is a very philosophical and very directed guide to the latest understandings in streamlined ("Agile") development. Other books go into more detail on particular subjects. The following list is meant to be used as a *pool* of books, to be read freely, in alternating fashion, in comfortable chunks. By the way, all of these books, except the first, are Addison-Wesley books.

- *The Object-Oriented Thought Process, Second Edition* (SAMS, 2003), by Matt Weisfeld, basically expands on and reiterates the bulk of Chapter Two.

- Next, despite its low-level-sounding name, *Object-Oriented Methods: Principles and Practice, Third Edition* (Addison-Wesley, 2000), by Ian Graham, provides extremely comprehensive coverage of the history and trends of function orientation approaches.

- *Design Patterns Explained: A New Perspective on Object-Oriented Design, Second Edition* (Addison-Wesley, 2004), by Alan Shalloway and James R. Trott, lays out a solid step-by-step approach to analyzing and designing through narrowing context, guided by interaction mechanism types.

- *Design Patterns: Elements of Reusable Object-Oriented Software* (Addison-Wesley, 1995), by Erich Gamma, Richard Helm, Ralph Johnson, and John Vlissides, is the cornerstone book on interaction mechanism types. It is very thorough and detailed, including about the meaning and uses of individual mechanism types. It also includes at least one fairly detailed code example for each, in C++ or Smalltalk. The interaction algebra examples in Chapter Four can also serve as a quick detailed catalog for the entire book, and each formula is actually a *map* for the corresponding code example. (There are also other "Design Patterns" books, by other authors, that have more-specialized interaction mechanism types.) For the most effective reading of *Design Patterns*, it's helpful to keep in mind that:

  - Its successive sections of an explanation often use differing names for the same entity.

  - Some sections don't note some parameters.

  - Some examples are spread over multiple sections.

  - Each benefits and consequences section doesn't identify which is which.

  - The book just barely predates UML, so its diagrams are not quite standard, but it does explain them inside the back cover.

- *Refactoring: Improving the Design of Existing Code* (Addison-Wesley, 1999), by Martin Fowler, addresses sound practices for the design optimization process. It is a pointed cross-check for other areas of designing that provides a very good feeling for the spectrum of class usages.

- And *Modern C++ Design: Generic Programming and Design Patterns Applied* (Addison-Wesley, 2001), by Andrei Alexandrescu, is the book that introduces the template-based, low-level designing technique. It is intense.

Untangled Web

It's easiest at this point to examine the range of aspects of one approach. The books listed here serve that purpose for Java. All of these are O'Reilly books. Each of the "in a Nutshell" series books is mostly a *reference* to the standard classes—just the *declaration* of their data items and functions—preceded by a *brief* description of their common usages. While that treatment is beneficial as an introduction only at a high level, it does provide a fairly quick detailed view of the scope of functions that the packages address.

- *JavaServer Faces* (O'Reilly, 2004), by Hans Bergsten, is a very thorough and well-thought-out explanation of the module-based approach to browser application development. It also addresses various compatibilities and conflicts with other technologies.

- *JavaServer Pages, Third Edition* (O'Reilly, 2003), also by Hans Bergsten, is a similar explanation of the technology that JavaServer Faces is an extension of. As such, it includes further details of that technology. The third edition is for JSP 2.0.

- *Java in a Nutshell, Fifth Edition* (O'Reilly, 2005), by David Flanagan, is dedicated to the more-basic global language functions. *Java Foundation Classes in a Nutshell* (O'Reilly, 1999), also by David Flanagan, covers the functions related to development of user interfaces. *Java Enterprise in a Nutshell, Second Edition* (O'Reilly, 2002), by Jim Farley, William Crawford, and David Flanagan, extends to the functions for servers and very large distributed applications.

Appendix A

This appendix describes how the Descript dialect *differs* from the D dialect.

Syntax of Descript

Descript has all of the syntactical clauses of, in the same order as (with one exception), D. But, instead of symbols and columns, it has **label**s. The only symbols allowed are arithmetical.

General Formats

Every line in a product, resource, or interval definition is a descriptive statement. There are up to three functional segments in each statement: the **component segment**, the **source segment**, and the **management segment**.

Each label is delimited by a colon and a space.

```
label: element
```

Multiple elements are separated by a semicolon and a space.

```
label1: element1; label2: element2
```

When a label is part of an element of another label, the first label does not need a colon.

```
label1 element1label: element1
```

A comment is denoted by a statement starting with the label `comment`.

```
comment: In normal writing, an asterisk indicates a note following its subject.
```

Some statements start with a keyword or keyphrase, delimited by a semicolon and a space, for context.

```
keyword; label: element
```

Management Definitions

An implicit library specification has the label library and the library name, followed by the label product set and one or more set names.

```
library: D : Math; product set: Circle
```

Each product part completion and resource part access implicit interval specification begins with the label store and the product name or resource name, respectively. This is followed by the label part and the part name. The intervals for completions and accesses can be centrally referenced, with the labels completion and access, respectively. (This statement's clause order is different from D.)

```
store: Keyed Report; part: Keyed Report Line;
   completion: Keyed Report Line Product;
   access: Keyed Report Line Resource
```

An in-set alias entry has the label alias and the alias interval set name, followed by the label translation and the translation.

```
alias: Option Selection; translation: selectOption
```

Major Definitions (Header Statements)

A characteristics definition is indicated by the label characteristics.

```
characteristics: temporary
```

A product's interval definition is denoted by a header statement that has the interval name following the label interval. It's followed by the interval's return component definition, which is the label return type, followed by a component type. If there is no return component, then that is denoted by a return type label with no return type.

```
interval: Picture Validation
   return type: bool
```

and

```
interval: Context Acquisition
   return type:
```

For a managed interval, each component definition is begun by the label label, for the interval's invocation, then each management component is used as a label. The component type follows the label type.

```
interval: Picture Validation;
  label: Width; type: int; label: Height; type: int
  return type: bool
```

Minor Definitions (Body Statements)

The first (component) segment can be a component definition, a component reference, or a product part reference.

The second, or source, segment can be a component reference (or an explicit value), a combination, or an interval reference. These are not allowed when the first segment has a product part reference.

The third segment—the management segment—can contain an incrementation designation, which is a resource reference or a resource part reference, or it can contain an arithmetic expression or an interval reference.

When either (or both) of the first two segments is non-null, and the third is a resource (or part) reference, this is a compound statement.

Component Definitions

A component definition has the label component and the component name, followed by the type label. A component type is optionally after the type label. An initial value is then optionally preceded by the label value.

```
component: Response; type:;
```

is equivalent to

```
component: Response; type: string; value: null
```

A component group definition has the label group and the component group name. This is followed by the group member component definitions, followed by a statement with just the keyphrase group end, all of which can be indented. Because of the allowed indentations here, each definition must be followed by a semicolon.

```
group: Keyed Report Line
    component: Sequence Number; type: smallint; value: 1
    type: smallint
    component: Department Number; type: smallint
    group end
```

A component series definition follows the group definition format, with the label series and the keyphrase series end, but the series name is optional; and an optional size name, preceded by the label size name and a size value, preceded by the label size value, are part of the series definition statement.

```
series: Report Page Spacing; size name: Lines Per Page;
  size value: 60;
  component: Character Count; type: smallint; value: 2;
  series end
```

and

```
series:; size name: Estimated Maximum Employees; size value: 100;
  component: Employee Number; type: int; series end
```

String definitions can follow the series format, except here simply the type string (or nothing) is the member definition, and the optional value clause applies to the entire series.

```
series: Status Message; size name: Characters Per Line;
  size value: 132;
  value: "Products were completed without incident."
```

translates to

```
series: Status Message; size value: 132; component: character;
  type: char;
  value: "Products were completed without incident."
```

Component References

A component reference has the component label and the component name.

```
component: Response
```

Any component reference can list multiple components, separated by commas.

```
component: Coordinates
```

can be

```
component: Last X, Last Y
```

A unique group member can be referenced by just its name. Any nonunique member must be preceded by all of its immediate owner levels until one of those is unique. This reference must begin with the group label and each level must be preceded by the label sublevel.

```
group: Original Report Line; sublevel: Print Control;
  component: Another Component
```

A series member reference must begin with the series label followed by all of its series levels, separated by commas, then the member. No specified series levels indicate all of the occurrences of the member.

```
series: Week Number, Employee Counter; component: Hours Worked
```

> and

```
series:; component: Hours Worked
```

When a series is in a group, or vice versa, a reference to a low-enough member requires a mixture of syntax. The series label is needed any time the level type switches to series. The group label is needed any time the level type switches to group. In a string reference, the character member is implied.

```
series: Response; group: Character Number
```

Source References

A source reference has the same labels as the component references, but the first label is prefixed with the label source. For source components, the standard is actually just the source label.

```
source component: Response
```

> translates to

```
source: Response

source group: Original Report Line; sublevel: Print Control;
  component: Another Component
```

> and

```
source series: Week Number, Employee Counter;
  component: Hours Worked
```

Combinations

Source combinations have just the source label.

```
component: Group Mark Column; source: Group End Column +
```

and

```
component: Group Begin Column; source: + Group Mark Column
```

and

```
component: Column Counter; source: +
```

and

```
component: Range Message; source: "The number is between"
  Low Number " and " High Number "."
```

Product Part References

A product part completion begins with the `completion` label and ends with the keyphrase `completion end`. Its simplest form has no product part processing statements.

```
completion: Report Line
comment: all of the components populated
completion end
```

and

```
comment: components populated in various places
completion: Report Line; completion end
```

Interval References

An interval reference is delineated by the label `jump`, followed by the interval label, followed by the interval name. Function intervals and extension intervals are referenced with their respective keyword preceding the interval label, just as in the definition. The interval label is only for clarifying.

```
jump: Attribute Check
```

and

```
component: Pixel Count; jump function: Picture Size
```

A managed interval reference has the management component names as labels.

```
component: Goal Number; type:;
  jump: Random Number; Low Number: 1; High Number: 100;
  Decimal Places: 0
```

Interval reference nesting is very clearly identified by a two-dimensional step. For the nested portion, in place of the component is the keyword nested. For the interval reference portion, in place of the nested interval reference is the keyword nesting.

```
nested; jump: string length; String: Original Value
component: Component Value; jump: string segment;
  String: Report Layout;
  Begin Position: Column Counter; End Position: nesting
```

Specific Usages

A specific usage is described with the label for followed by a condition.

```
jump: Header Skip; for: Print Control = Page Break
```

The condition controls are the labels and and with. Parentheses are used for grouping.

```
jump: Group Code Process; Group Type: Group Type;
  for: Group Fields;
  with: (Column Counter = Group Begin Column;
    and: Column Counter = Group End Column +)
```

A parallel specific usage condition is designated by each of the involved statements starting with the keyword parallel.

```
parallel; jump: Main Line Process; for: Special Attribute
  = Main Line Attribute
parallel; jump: Redefine Process; for: Special Attribute
  = Redefine Attribute
parallel; jump: Table Process; for: others
```

Resource Part References

A resource part access has the access label.

```
access: Report Line
```

Repetitions

A repetition is described with the appended label for every, followed by a condition.

```
for every: Print Control \= Double Space;
  access: Report Original Line
```

Instead of a resource access, the Rrepetitions notation can be an arithmetic operator and incrementation amount or a nonreturn interval reference.

```
for every: Column Counter \> Line Width; source: Column Counter + 1
```

Specific Blocks

Specific usages and incrementations can have immediate follow-up steps. Each of these starts with the keyphrase follow up.

```
component: Source Code; source: Empty Layout Message;
  for: Source Code = Not Written
follow up; part: Source Code
```

Status Management

Status monitoring has two forms: single statement monitoring and multiple statement monitoring. The multiple form starts with the keyphrase monitor on for an on or the keyphrase monitor off for an off, and the single form starts with the keyphrase monitor next. These keyphrases can be the keywords on, off, and next, respectively.

```
monitor next; part: Unexpected End of File;
  for: status = End of File
```

and

```
on; part: Unexpected End of File; for: End of File
```

and

```
off; for: End of File
```

Interval Orientation

The first line is simply the label parent and the name of the parent class.

```
parent: Shape
```

An implementation of an interface-only has the label "*interface*", followed by one or more interface-only class names, separated by commas.

```
interface: Error, Message
```

An object definition has the component label and the label object—and, optionally, the label locater—and the object name. This is followed by the type label—and, optionally, the label class—and the class name. A generalized object is denoted by the label ancestor and an ancestor name, between the two other entities. This is followed by a reference to an initialization interval, implicitly of the class. A specializable type is denoted by the keyword specializable preceding the the type label.

```
component object: Shape; ancestor: Shape; type: Circle;
  jump: initialization; Radius: Radius
```

An object reference is denoted by the object label followed by the object name. A class reference is denoted by the class label followed by the class name. A library reference has the library label followed by the library name. Again, any interval reference begins with the jump label; here, the interval label is required.

```
component: Radius; jump object: Focus Circle; interval: Radius
```

and

```
component: Area; jump library: D : Math; class: Circle;
  interval: Area; Radius: Radius
```

A type change is denoted by a component reference followed by the label new type and the new type, followed by the source.

```
component: Focus Shape; new type: Circle; source: Previous Shape
```

Interaction Properties

The usability is defined with the label usability.

```
component: Pi; type:; usability: any; value: 3.14159
```

and

```
interval: Area; label: Radius; type: float
  return type: float; usability: any
```

The rigidity is defined with the label rigidity.

```
component: Pi; type:; usability: any; rigidity: execution;
  value: 3.14159
```

and

```
interval: Area; label: Radius; type: float
  return type: float; usability: any; rigidity: execution
```

A variable component's usability can be only self, so the self keyword is not specified. Implicit standard access and update intervals can be designated with the out and in keywords, respectively, separated by a comma, as the usability.

```
component: Radius; type: float; usability: in, out; rigidity: variable;
```

and

```
component: Radius; type: float; usability: in; rigidity: variable;
```

and

```
component: Radius; type: float; usability: out; rigidity: variable;
```

and

```
component: Radius; type: float; usability:; rigidity: variable;
```

A block interval can be designated as the usability, with the added jump label and referencing interval name.

```
interval: Area; label: Radius; type: float
  return type: float; usability: jump: Shape Statistics; rigidity: execution
```

Advanced Elements

Chaining is possible with the two-dimensional nesting step. For the object creation portion, in place of the object name is the nested keyword. For the interval reference portion, in place of the object creation is the nesting keyword.

```
nested; jump class: Circle; interval: initialization; Radius: New Radius
jump object: nesting; interval: Rendering
```

Locations cannot be compared with the equal sign; they must be compared with either of two generic intervals: "same object as", which is implemented (in generic) with the equal sign, or "equivalent to", which is an empty interval, because it's different for each class. For ease of use, these generic intervals can be referenced with standard label syntax.

```
component: Same Values Count; source: +;
  for object: Current Object = object: Desired Object
```

is illegal.

```
component: Same Values Count; source: +;
  for object: Current Object; equivalent to: Desired Object
```

is clear and is equivalent to

```
component: Same Values Count; source: +;
  for jump object: Current Object; interval: equivalent to;
  other object: Desired Object
```

and

```
component: Same Object Count; source: +;
  for object: Current Object; same object as: Desired Object
```

is equivalent to

```
component: Same Object Count; source: +;
  for jump object: Current Object; interval: same object as;
  other object: Desired Object
```

An inner class is defined with a header statement of the label inner class and the inner class name. It is referenced with the label inner and the inner class name.

```
inner class: Mouse Monitor
```

and

```
jump inner: Mouse Monitor
```

and

```
jump class: Inquiry Form; inner: Mouse Monitor
```

An interval location is copied with the label location added to the interval label.

```
component object: Action Monitor; source interval location: Action Performed
```

Aspect Orientation

The called interval has inlet names, each preceded by the label inlet, to mark the inlet. And the call is continued with the keyword injections. The injection begins with the label injection and injection name followed by the statements to inject. And the call is ended with the keyphrase injections end on a line by itself.

```
interval: Server Interval
comment: some core statements
inlet: Security -- Login
comment: more core statements
```

```
interval: Client Interval
jump object: Server; interval: Server Interval; injections
injection: Security -- Login
jump object: Third-party; interval: User Validation
injections end
```

Injections can be in an interval outside of an interval reference. Any noninjection code must be marked by a preceding line that is just the injections end keyphrase. They can stand alone or in a group, in an injection set, denoted by a file name prefixed with injection set. It is referred to (functionally copied), anywhere in a class or other injection set, with the label injection set and the nonprefixed injection set name.

```
injection set: Security
```

Reserved Words

Obviously, Descript relies very little on punctuation and very much on words, so it has many more reserved words than D.

Labels

Individual Identifiers

access	inner class	product set
alias	interface	return type
ancestor	interval	rigidity
characteristics	jump	size name
class	label	size value
comment	library	source
completion	locater	store
component	location	sublevel
injection	new type	translation
injection set	object	type
inlet	parent	usability
inner	part	value

Controls

and	for	same object as
equivalent to	for every	set return

Keyphrases

Scopes

completion end	monitor next	next
follow up	monitor off	off
group end	monitor on	on
injections	nested	parallel
injections end	nesting	series end

Controls

return	set return

Modifiers

addition	function	removal
all opposite	incomplete	replacement
aspect	interface only	restart
extension	last	specialized
finish	or	start
first	others	

Property Values

any	execution	self
ascendants	library	temporary
definition	permanent	variable

General Values

false	null	parent
initialization	object	true

Appendix B

This appendix describes the *additional* features of the Desc dialect.

Syntax of Desc

The simplest explanation of Desc's syntax is that it allows the column separators and punctuation of D, and the labels and added keyphrases of Descript. The punctuation can be used *in place* of any of the corresponding keywords, but they cannot both be used for the same element. In Desc, the *reserved* labels do not require the colon, and all of the reserved words and managed interval labels can be abbreviated. The abbreviations can be as short as the least number of leading letters that distinguish each reserved word. Additionally, there are specific abbreviations, which especially facilitate the most-used reserved words.

Also, in Desc, the layered interval references don't need inner left punctuation; the left angle bracket is still required, though. Even with this shortcut, the layers are still visually obvious.

```
Radius | <Focus Circle) Radius>
```

and

```
Area | <D : Math} Circle] Area : Radius>
```

So, Desc can be as long as pure Descript and as short as shorter than D—D with abbreviated keywords (and symbols). It's actually all three dialects—and all of the possible combinations of them.

In addition to all of the elements of D and Descript, Desc has one other element, because of the ability to abbreviate interval labels. In the managed interval definition, each management component can have a specific abbreviation defined, in parentheses or with the label abbreviation, following the component name. While this is a nice feature, it's also important for ongoing development; when a new label makes an existing label's leading-letter abbreviation indistinguishable, and that abbreviation is widely used, the specific abbreviation can be assigned to the existing label, and no further changes will be required.

```
<Picture Validation : Width (W) [int] | : Height (H) [int] |>
  [bool]
```

is equivalent to

```
interval: Picture Validation; label: Width; abbreviation: W;
  type: int; label: Height; abbreviation: H; type: int;
  purpose return type: bool
```

Reserved Words

In the following sections, the distinguishing letters are in italics. Also, the second column lists the specific abbreviations. Italics in an abbreviation mean that it can be as short as those letters. The same abbreviation can be for both a label and a keyphrase; this is possible because of the context (placement) in a statement.

Labels

Individual Identifiers

*ac*cess
*al*ias
*anc*estor
*cl*ass
*ch*aracteristics
*comm*ent   cm
*compl*etion
*compo*nent   com
group
injection   inj
injection set   injs
*inl*et
inner   inn
inner class   inc
*interf*ace
*interv*al   inter
jump
*la*bel   l
*li*brary
*locate*r   lo
*locati*on

*n*ew type

*o*bject

*par*ent

part

*pr*oduct set   ps

*pur*pose

*ret*urn type   rt

*ri*gidity

*se*ries

*size n*ame   sn

*size v*alue   sv

*so*urce   s

*st*ore

*su*blevel

*tr*anslation

*ty*pe

*u*sability

*v*alue

Controls

and   *a*n

*eq*uivalent to

for   *fo*

*for e*very   fe

*sa*me object as

*w*ith

Keyphrases

Scopes

*c*ompletion end   ce

*fo*llow up

*gr*oup end   ge

injections   injs

*injections e*nd   injse

*monitor n*ext   mx

*monitor of*f   mf

monitor on   mn

*neste*d	ne
*nesti*ng	ni
*nex*t	nx
*of*f	
on	
*para*llel	pa
*seri*es end	se

Controls

*ret*urn	r
set return	sr

Modifiers

*ad*dition	
*al*l opposite	ao
*asp*ect	
*ext*ension	
*fin*ish	
*fir*st	
*inc*omplete	
*int*erface only	ifo
*la*st	
or	
*ot*hers	
*rem*oval	rm
*rep*lacement	rp
*res*tart	
*st*art	

Property Values

*an*y	
*asc*endants	
*def*inition	
*exec*ution	
*li*brary	
*per*manent	
*sel*f	
*tem*porary	
*v*ariable	

General Values

*fa*lse

*ini*tialization

*nu*ll

*ob*ject   o

*pare*nt   p

*tru*e

An Example of Desc

The following is the same fairly simple interval set as the example of D. Various formats are used in the short code, to demonstrate the flexibility, but, with Desc, any company should set consistency standards.

Listing B-1. *The Guessing Game, in D*

```
> Application

-- permanent --
<application : parameter count [int] : parameters <> [string]>
  [] any
(Guessing Game) [Guessing Game] | <initialization>

-- temporary --

<Guessing Game>
  [Guessing Game]
Another Round | "y"
Response [string] variable
| <Round> | for every Response = Another Round

<Round>
Goal Number [smallint] | <[Number] Random Number : 1 : 100 : 0>
Player Number [] variable | 0
| <To Screen : "Guess my number.">
Low Number [] variable | 1
High Number [] variable | 100
| <Clue> | for every Player Number \= Goal Number
| <To Screen : "Right.  Do you want to play again?">
Response | <From Screen>

<Clue>
| <To Screen : "The number is from "
  Low Number " to " High Number ".  Your guess:">
Player Number | <From Screen>
| <To Screen : "Higher."> | for Player Number < Goal Number
+ Low Number | Player Number + | for Player Number \< Low Number
| <To Screen : "Lower."> | for Player Number > Goal Number
+ High Number | Player Number - | for Player Number \> High Number
```

Listing B-2. *The Guessing Game, in Desc*

```
ancestor Application

-- permanent
<application : parameter count [int] : parameters <> [string]>
  [] any
(Guessing Game) [Guessing Game] | <initialization>

char: temporary

<initialization>
  purpose: [Guessing Game]
Another Round | "y"
Response; type: string
| <Round> | for every Response = Another Round

int: Round
component: Goal Number [smallint]; jump: Random Number; Low: 1 : 100 DP: 0
c: Player Number; t:y | 0
j: To Screen : "Guess my number."
comp: Low Number; ty:; v: 1
com High Number; typ; val 100
j Clue | for every Player Number \= Goal Number
| j To Screen; String: "Right.  Do you want to play again?"
c Response; j From Screen

i Clue
j To Screen : "The number is from "
  Low Number " to " High Number ".  Your guess:"
Player Number | <From Screen>
| j: To Screen : "Higher."; f: Player Number < Goal Number
+ Low Number | Player Number +; f Player Number \< Low Number
| <To Screen : "Lower."> | (Player Number > Goal Number)
f; c High Number; s Player Number -; f Player Number \> High Number
```

Appendix C

This translation key can be used just for quick reference, or in conjunction with the data-oriented dictionary.

Procedure-Oriented to Data-Oriented Translation Key

The procedure-oriented vocabulary here is most closely related to Java.

Concepts

abstract class incomplete class
abstract method interface-only interval
address location
arithmetic operation combination
array series
block follow-up steps
calculation combination
call jump
cast type change
class interval set
class member permanent characteristic
concatenation combination
data declaration component definition
data item component
data name component reference
data type component type
dynamic member temporary characteristic
for loop incrementation set
function interval
function data item interval component
function orientation interval orientation
if conditional specific usage

import library implicit reference
instance member temporary characteristic
interface interface-only class
library package
main method application interval
message interval reference
method interval
method data item interval component
object member temporary characteristic
object orientation interval orientation
package product line
parameter management component
program product set
read resource part access
record part
reference locater
static member permanent characteristic
structure group
switch parallel specific usage
tokenized string incomplete string
type component type
while loop repetition
write product part completion

Keyphrases

and with
close finish
delete removal
else for others
final execution (component), definition (interval)
if for
open start
or and
private self
protected ascendants
public any
rewrite replacement
static permanent
this object
while for every
write addition

Data-Oriented Dictionary

In the descriptions, any bold words are also defined in this dictionary. For brevity, any syntax descriptions are most closely related to D.

access

When not modified by or modifying other words, a **resource part access**.

access interval

An **interval** that allows access to a self variable component. An interval name that matches a noninterval component name, without parameters; or an interval name that matches a noninterval collection name, with one parameter.

addition

A normal product part completion.

alias

An entity to implicitly translate a noun-based **interval** to another language's corresponding verb-based method name. A **statement** of the alias interval name enclosed in angle brackets, followed by the translation.

```
<Option Selection> selectOption
```

alias table

A table of **aliases**, outside of any **set**.

ancestry statement

A **set statement** that describes the **set's** complete ancestry, in reverse order, for both definition and documentation. A greater-than sign at the beginning of the **statement** and preceding each successive ancestor.

> Shape > View

aspect class

A fundamental class that each other class must ascend from, to serve clearer purpose. Denoted by aspect as the first statement, instead of an **ancestry statement** (because the **generic class** is the only ancestor of an aspect class), the standard aspect classes are "language"; "Utility", "Mediation", and "Application"; and "View", "Model", "Security", "Logging", and "Persistence".

aspect orientation

To specifically separate (auxiliary) things like security and logging logic from the (core) business logic. Employs **inlets** into an interval, and **injections** from a referencing interval, based on matching the name of the inlet and the injection, causing only these to require a naming standard. Serves as a reverse reference for the server interval, extending a longtime technique—passing a service object—to the interval level.

block interval

A self interval referenced by a single interval, designated, in the interval definition, to use the referencing interval's components directly. Logically, a block of the referencing interval, also reflects more-specific usability than self.

body statement

A **statement** that does not define the scope of other statements. Its scope is defined by a **header statement**.

chaining

Object creation solely for the purpose of an **interval reference** in the same step. Possible with the two-dimensional **nesting statement**.

```
^ [Circle] | <initialization : Radius>
| <^ Rendering>
```

characteristic

Any entity of an **interval set**, either **permanent** or **temporary**.

characteristics set

One of two sets of entities of an **interval set**, either **permanent** or **temporary**.

column

A physical segment of a **statement**, to serve generic functionality, it's variable width, separated by a vertical slash from the adjoining column. The **component column**, the **source column**, or the **control column**.

combination

Two or more **components** combined through one or more arithmetic or string operations, the same as Java-based assignments, with a few exceptions.

```
Group Mark Column | Group End Column +
```

and

```
Group Begin Column | + Group Mark Column
```

and

```
Column Counter | +
```

and

```
Result Message | "The next valid transaction "
    "number is " Transaction Main Number & Transaction Check Digits
```

comment

A non-code **statement**. Starts with an asterisk.

```
* In normal writing, an asterisk indicates a note following its subject.
```

completion

When not modified by or modifying other words, a **product part completion**.

component

Any smallest practical piece of a **product**, **resource**, or **interval set**. Also the generic term for a group or a series.

component column

The first **column** of a **statement**.

component definition

A **statement** with the **component** name followed by brackets, optionally enclosing a **component type**, in the first column, and an initial value optionally in the second column, followed by the **interaction properties**.

```
Response [string] | null
```

component group

A set of any **components** (or **series** or other groups).

component list

A **component reference** to multiple **components**, separated by commas.

component name preword

A component name prefix separated by a space, to make less frequent purposes more immediately obvious. One of three values identifying which type of definition the component is (directly) defined in—permanent, temporary, or management—with p, t, and m, respectively; and one of three other values identifying how the component is used—that it's a variable, dynamic string, or incomplete string—with v, d, and i, respectively. The two categories can be combined into one preword, with the definition identification first.

```
v Radius [float] (in, out) variable
```

    and

```
p Pi [] any execution | 3.14159
```

    and

```
tv Old Length [] self variable
```

    and

```
<Area : m Radius [float]>
```

component segment

In Descript, the first **segment** of a **statement**.

component series

A set of multiple occurrences of the same **component** (or **group** or other series).

component type

The format and functionality of a **component**.

compound statement

A **statement** in which either or both of the first two **columns** have something and the third does also. Part of a compound statement controls the rest of it.

constant component

A **component** with a value, specifically to allow symbolic values to not be used in **step statements**, forcing purpose to be as clear as possible.

continuation

In a multiline **statement**, an indentation on each succeeding line.

continuation mark

In a multiline **statement** that contains other multiline statements (for example, a **group definition**), a semicolon at the end of a continued line of a contained statement.

control column

The third **column** of a **statement**.

control incrementation

An **access**, or a specialized **component** incrementation or **interval reference**. Just the incrementation component followed by an arithmetic operator and an incrementation amount, or a reference to an interval that cannot return a component.

control segment

In Descript, the third **segment** of a **statement**.

durability (interaction property)

Simply defined by which characteristics set the component definition or interval definition is in.

dynamic string

A string that has an implicit construction when referenced. Compared to an **incomplete string**, it doesn't require a **component list** when referenced.

dynamic string definition

A string **component definition** with a single set of angle brackets and a standard string construction.

```
Availability Message [] | <> "The room is available on " Target Date
  ", from " Start Time " to " End Time "."
```

extension interval

A feature that functionally promotes **interval components**, specifically to allow using a referenced **interval** to create **components** for the referencing interval—effectively, a referencing interval inheriting from a referenced interval. Denoted by the left angle bracket preceded by extension or an exclamation mark with no space.

```
!<Context Acquisition>
```

finish

The finish to processing on a **product** or **resource**, usually implied.

follow-up step

A step that is executed to accommodate the true condition of the step before it, forming a single-level functional block.

follow-up step definition

A **statement** that starts with a plus sign.

```
[Source Code || (Source Code = Not Written)
+ Source Code | Empty Layout Message |
+ ]
```

function interval

An **interval** whose sole purpose is to produce its **return component**, denoted by the left angle bracket preceded by function or a question mark without a space following it.

```
?<Picture Size>
```

generalized object

An object defined as one type and initialized as a specialization of that type. Denoted by an ancestor, enclosed in brackets, between the two other entities.

```
(User Shape) [Shape] [Circle] | <initialization : Radius>
```

generic (class)

The most basic class, from which all other classes are extended.

group

When not modified by or modifying other words, a **component group**.

group alignment member

A **group member** with no member component name.

group definition

A **statement** with the component group name and the left bracket; followed by the
component definition of each **group member** and a statement with just the right
bracket, all of which can be indented.

```
Keyed Report Line [
    Sequence Number [smallint] | 1
    [smallint]
    Department Number [smallint]
    ]
```

group member

A **component** that is part of a **group**.

group member reference

For a unique group member, just its name; for a nonunique member, the member
name preceded by all of its immediate owner levels' name until one of those is unique.
This reference must begin with group or an at sign, the levels must be separated by
colons, and all of it must be enclosed in angle brackets.

```
<@ Original Report Line : Print Control : Another Component>
```

header statement

A **statement** that defines the scope of **body statements**.

idiom

Code that doesn't properly translate to another language—a rare occurrence—remains
intact, to help to ensure complete compatibility. Designated with a backslash in the first
column; effectively a comment that gets its comment character stripped.

implementation statement

A **set statement** that defines all of the **interface-only classes** that the **set** implements. A double greater-than sign at the beginning of the **statement**, followed by one or more interface-only class names, separated by commas.

```
>> Error, Message
```

implicit access

The standard (single statement) access **interval**, designated in the **component definition**. Designated with in enclosed in parentheses, in place of the usability property. Can be combined with **implicit update**.

```
Radius [float] (in, out) variable
```

implicit update

The standard (single statement) update **interval**, designated in the **component definition**. Designated with out enclosed in parentheses, in place of the usability property. Can be combined with **implicit access**.

```
Radius [float] (in, out) variable
```

incomplete class

A class that has any, but not all, **interface-only intervals**. Identified with just incomplete as its second statement.

incomplete string

A string that has **component** insertion points. Compared to a **dynamic string**, its definition is functionally completed when referenced.

incomplete string definition

A string **component definition** with a set of angle brackets with nothing between them for each **component** insertion point.

```
Availability Message [] | "The room is available on <>, from <> to <>."
```

incomplete string reference

A **component list** of the string name and the insertion string components, in order.

incrementation set

A **repetition** implemented in conjunction with a **control incrementation**. Can include a **specific usage**.

```
|| {Print Control \= Double Space} Report Original Line
```

injection

A direct or indirect addition to an **interval reference**, to add logic to the referenced interval. In the direct form, the reference without a right angle bracket, its statement followed by an injection header, which has the injection name enclosed in double angle brackets, followed by the statements to inject, followed by the interval reference's right angle bracket on a line by itself.

```
<Client Interval>
| <(Server) Server Interval
<<Security -- Login>>
| <(Third-Party) User Validation>
>
```

injection set

A set of **injections** that stand alone or in a group. Denoted by a file name with a caret prefix, referred to (functionally copied) anywhere in a class or other injection set, with the injection set name, including the caret, enclosed in double angle brackets.

```
<<^ Security>>
```

inlet

A point in an **interval** where an **injection** can add logic. In the referenced interval, an inlet name, surrounded by double angle brackets, in the second column.

```
<Server Interval>
* some core statements
| <<Security -- Login>>
* more core statements
```

interaction properties

Definitions of how any entity interacts with other entities. **Usability**, **rigidity**, and **durability**.

interface-only class

A class that has all **interface-only intervals**. Identified with just interface only as its first **statement**.

interface-only interval

An **interval** that has no implementation. Identified with just interface only in its body.

interval

A description of **components** through a period of time.

interval component

A **component** that is defined in an **interval definition**.

interval definition

A **header statement** that has the **interval** name enclosed in angle brackets, followed by the interval's **return component definition**, followed by the **interaction properties**.

```
<Picture Validation>
  [bool]
```

interval locater

The explicit term for a **locater** that contains the location of an **interval**; can also be called just a locater. Copied with the standard **interval reference** enclosed in parentheses.

```
(Action Monitor) | (<Action Performed>)
```

interval orientation

The organization of groups of steps into functional units, specifically to make the groups more independent of each other, to help to minimize code changes.

interval reference (fully explicit)

A visual representation of the layering, as opposed to a stringing. Within angle brackets, with **function intervals** and **extension intervals** having their respective keywords or punctuation; an object name enclosed in parentheses and any entity name; or a line name enclosed in braces, a class name enclosed in brackets, and any entity name. With an **interval locater**, the same as with an object locater, without a further interval name.

```
Radius | ?<(Focus Circle) Radius>
```

and

```
Area | ?<[{D : Math} Circle] Area : Radius>
```

and

```
| <(Action Monitor) : Action>
```

interval set

A description of **products** and, more directly, their **components** through periods of time (**intervals**).

jump

Triggered by an **interval reference**, a change of flow from within one **interval** to the beginning of another, through that one and back to the statement that follows the reference. Delineated by the interval name enclosed in angle brackets in the second column.

```
Pixel Count | ?<Picture Size>
```

keyphrase

A keyword, or a specific set of keywords separated by spaces, that isn't a **label**. All lower-case, to easily differentiate them from developer-defined words, which are title cased.

label

A word, or a specific set of words separated by spaces, that describes what an entity is, as opposed to how it is used. These can be reserved or developer defined.

line

When not modified by or modifying other words, or when used in "in a line" (as opposed to "on a line"), a **product line**.

line implicit reference

A **statement** at the beginning of a set to allow **set references** to imply their **line reference**. A line reference, followed by every applicable referenced set name, separated by commas.

```
{D : Math} Circle
```

list

When not modified by or modifying other words, a **component list**.

locater

A **component** containing the location of another component, for an object or **interval** only, and most simply thought of as the object or interval itself. Used exactly like any other component, except its value can't be set explicitly.

major entity

An entity that defines the scope of **minor entities**, defined by a collection of **statements**. A **characteristics set** or an **interval**.

managed interval

An **interval** that operates on or from one or more **management components**.

managed interval definition

An interval definition that includes a management component definition list.

```
<Picture Validation : Width [int] | : Height [int] |>
  [bool]
```

managed interval reference (recommended format)

The **managed interval reference short format**, with a **label** before each colon, and a semicolon before each label.

```
Goal Number [] |
  ?<Random Number; Low Number: 1; High Number: 100; Decimal Places: 0>
```

managed interval reference (short format)

The interval name, followed by the **management component** values or other **component** names, each preceded by a colon.

```
Goal Number [] | ?<Random Number : 1 : 100 : 0>
```

management component

A subject or a controller of a **managed interval**.

management component definition

A list with each component definition preceded by a colon and the optional value being a default value.

```
<Picture Validation : Width [int] | : Height [int] |>
```

minor entity

Any non-**major entity**, which doesn't define the scope of other entities. A **part**, a **component**, a **group**, or a **series**.

multicomponent return

A return of multiple **components**, which can be copied to either a group or a list.

nesting

One interval reference inside of another. In the two-dimensional form, for the nested portion, in place of the component is a caret, and for the interval reference portion, in place of the nested interval reference is another caret.

```
Component Value | ?<string segment : Report Layout
  : Column Counter : ?<string length : Original Value>>
```

and

```
^ | ?<string length : Original Value>
Component Value | ?<string segment : Report Layout
  : Column Counter : ^>
```

noninterval component

A **component** that is defined outside of an **interval**.

object definition

In its basic form, the object name enclosed in parentheses, followed by the class name enclosed in brackets, in the first column, and initialization as an interval reference, in the second column. In other forms, defines a **generalized object** or a **specialized type**.

```
(User Shape) [Circle] | <initialization : Radius>
```

package

A basically self-sufficient logical grouping of **product lines**.

parallel

When not modified by or modifying other words, a **parallel specific usage**.

parallel specific usage

A set of **specific usages** in which only the first true condition is accommodated, designated by each of the involved statements starting with a hyphen.

```
- | <Main Line Process> | for Special Attribute = Main Line Attribute
- | <Redefine Process> | for Special Attribute = Redefine Attribute
- | <Table Process> | for others
```

part

Any most practical subset of a **product** or a **resource**.

part implicit reference

A **statement** after any **line implicit reference** statements to allow an **interval** reference to stand out as a **completion** or **access**. Optionally, the completion interval name enclosed in angle brackets in the first column; the store name and the part name, separated by a colon, enclosed in brackets in the second column; and, optionally, the access interval name enclosed in angle brackets in the third column.

```
<Keyed Report Line Product> | [Keyed Report : Keyed Report Line]
   | <Keyed Report Line Resource>
```

permanent (characteristic)

Basically, an entity that can be shared directly with other **sets**.

permanent characteristics definition

A **statement** that is a double hyphen, followed by permanent, optionally followed by another double hyphen.

```
-- permanent --
```

product

An output of a system; the focus of data orientation.

product line

A logical collection of **sets**, to delineate related basic functionality.

product part completion

An occurrence of an output from a system. A left bracket and **product part** name in
the first column; in its recommended form, a right bracket in its own statement; in the
simpler form, the right bracket immediately following the part name.

```
[Report Keyed Line
* all of the components populated
]
```

and

```
* components populated in various places
[Report Keyed Line]
```

product set

An interval set.

reference

An entity usage, as opposed to an entity definition.

reflection

Examination of the **characteristics** of an object or a class. Two parts, a "class" **interval**,
which returns the name of the class of the object, and a "reflection" object, which can
be created with any string, can be combined.

```
User Class [string] | <(User Object) class>
Object Documentation [reflection] | User Class
```

can be combined into

```
Object Documentation [reflection] | <(User Object) class>
```

removal

A **product part completion** that is the removal of a part.

repetition

Similar to a **specific usage**, a process step based on a condition that occurs repeatedly, most often implemented in an **incrementation set**. Described with the sequence control `for every` followed by a condition, which can also be braces surrounding the condition.

```
|| {Print Control \= Double Space} Report Original Line
```

replacement

A **product part completion** that is the replacement of a part.

resource

An input for a system, which can also be seen as an intermediate output, either from the same system or another.

resource part access

An occurrence of an input to a system. Just the name of the **resource** (or resource **part**) in the third column.

```
|| Original Report
```

restart

A **finish** and then a **start**, appropriate for getting the **part** pointer set back to the beginning.

return component

A **component** that is returned from an **interval**. Its name is the same as the interval's by default.

return component definition

Part of an **interval definition**, on its own line, the return component's name (optionally) and type enclosed in brackets in the first column, and an initial value optionally in the second column.

```
[bool] | false
```

return multicomponent definition

A **return component definition** for a **multicomponent return**, it must include names, and its individual return components are separated by commas.

```
X [int] | 0, Y [int] | 0
```

rigidity (interaction property)

Determines when the entity being defined can be updated. Defined with any one of `definition`, `execution`, or `variable`, following the **usability** specification, if it exists.

segment

In Descript, a logical segment of a **statement**, to serve generic functionality; the **component segment**, the **source segment**, or the **control segment**.

sequence modification

A **specific usage** or a **repetition**—or both, which function as a selective grouping.

series

When not modified by or modifying other words, a **component series**.

series definition

A **statement** that follows the **group definition** format, but with the series name optional, and an optional size name and a size value, separated by a vertical slash, enclosed in angle brackets, preceding the left (square) bracket.

```
Report Page Spacing <Lines Per Page | 60> [Character Count [smallint] | 2]
```

and

```
<Estimated Maximum Employees | 100> [Employee Number [int]]
```

series member

A **component** that is part of a **series**.

series member reference

`series` or a number sign, followed by all of its series level indices' name, separated by commas, then a colon; and then the member name. Or no specified series levels, indicating all of the occurrences of the member, which is useful when the series is unnamed.

```
<# Week Number, Employee Counter : Hours Worked>
```

and

```
<# : Hours Worked>
```

set

When not modified by or modifying other words, an **interval set**.

set property

A basic set definition, documentation, or a shortcut. A **line implicit reference**, a **part implicit reference**, or an **alias**.

side effect

A self-contained standard comment that doesn't affect the statement at all, to make the statement stand out visually. Denoted with a slash as the first character, which is the comment.

```
/ active body statement
```

source column

The second **column** of a **statement**.

source segment

In Descript, the second **segment** of a **statement**.

specializable type

A feature that creates an object whose exact **type** is not determined until usage. Denoted with the ancestor name enclosed in parentheses inside of the brackets. This can be of any specificity, all the way down to generic.

```
(User Shape) [(Shape)] | <initialization : Radius>
```

specific usage

A process step based on a condition, with condition controls (and, with, and others) that describe all of the conditions that that step applies to. In the third column, for followed by a condition, or a condition enclosed in parentheses.

```
| <Header Skip> | (Print Control = Page Break)
| <Layout Check : Symbol Count> | for others
```

start

The start to processing on a **product** or **resource**, usually implied.

statement

A description of any set property or characteristic of an interval set; a set statement, a header statement, or a body statement.

status monitoring

On-and-off (functional block) status management, it has two forms: single **statement** monitoring and multiple statement monitoring. In the multiple form, a left brace for an on or a right brace for an off, followed by a `for` clause that can be applied to an implied "status" component and an implied status value component name, with `status =` optional; in the single form, both braces, then the `for` clause.

```
{} Unexpected End of Resource || for status = End of Resource
```

is a single.

```
{ Unexpected End of Resource || (End of Resource)
```

is on, and

```
} || (End of Resource)
```

is off.

status table

To serve **status** monitoring, a table for developer-defined status name, type (information, warning, error, or severe), and description, manually maintained, in a file named "status table".

step

A logical step of progression through a process.

step definition

Nearly every **body statement**, a description of a logical step of progression through a process; a baseline, nonorganizational description.

temporary (characteristic)

Basically, a characteristic that can be shared directly between **intervals**.

temporary characteristics definition

A **statement** that is a double hyphen, followed by temporary, optionally followed by another double hyphen.

```
-- temporary --
```

transitional code

A double comment that signifies that a design decision has not been made, to facilitate concise working notes in the code. Separating two statements, or, which can also be a question mark.

```
Line Position | +
? Line Position | + Field Length
```

type

When not modified by or modifying other words, a **component type**.

type change

The translation of a **component** from one **type** to another. Denoted by a component reference in the first column and the new type, enclosed in brackets, preceding the source in the second column.

```
(Focus Shape) | [Circle] (Previous Shape)
```

update interval

An **interval** that allows update of a `self variable` component. An interval name that matches a noninterval component name, with parameters; or an interval name that matches a noninterval collection name, with multiple parameters.

usability (interaction property)

Determines what types of entities can use the entity being defined. Defined with any one of `any`, `line`, `ascendants`, or `self`, following the component type or the return component definition.

Index

Symbols

@ sign, 100
& ampersand, 101
< > angle brackets, 95–98, 102
* asterisk, 95
\ backslash, 96
\\ double backslashes, 96
{ } braces/curly brackets, 106
^ caret, 104
, comma, 99, 100
: colon, 97, 100
- hyphen, 93
-- double hyphens, 93
- minus sign, 101
number sign, 100
+ plus sign, 101, 108
; semicolon, 98
[ ] square brackets, 98, 102
_ underscore, 104
| vertical slash, 93

Numbers

3-tier architecture, 43, 51, 52, 59

A

abstract classes, 6, 8
abstract functions, 30
access interval, 95, 112
action elements, 65
adaptability, 35
adaptation, 35
aggregation, 32
algebraic notation for object interactions, 71–86
alias table, 95
aliases, 46
all opposite keyphrase, 105
ampersand (&), 101
analysis, bidirectional, 26
ancestry statement, 110
anchor tags, 54
angle brackets (< >), 95–98, 102
Ant, 62
Apple Computer, 20
applets, 58
Application-ascendant classes, 117
application deployment descriptors, 64
application orientation, xxvi, 3-5
application servers, 58

applications
    managed via XML, 61
    tracking execution with diagnostic tools, 27
aspect orientation, 87
    in D, 115–17
    in Descript, 139
assertions, 62
associated methods, 31
asterisk (*), 95
at sign (@), 100
AT&T, 20
attributes, 32
automation, 88

B

backslash (\), 96
base class, 8
bidirectional analysis/design, 26, 37
binding, 31, 33
    C++ template feature and, 42
block languages, 6
blocking, 108
body statements, 92, 96, 98–109
braces ({ }), 106
brackets
    angle (< >), 95–98, 102
    curly ({ }), 106
    square ([ ]), 98, 102
branching, 48, 90
browser plug-ins, 56
browsers, 52–57
    added interaction capabilities in, 55–57
    formatting and, 53
    page variability in, 59
    processing flows and, 55
business objects, 63
buttons, 50
byte code, 58

C

C#, 21
C++, 12
    binding and, 33
    vs. Java, 18
    template feature of, 42
caret (^), 104
Cascading Style Sheets (CSS), 53, 57
casting, 16

chaining, 114
characteristics definitions, 96, 113
characteristics sets, 92, 113
class data, 29
.class extension, 57
class functions, 11, 29
class objects, 11
classes, 7
    abstract, 6, 8
    concrete, 6, 8
    derived, 6, 8
    designing, 39–41
    documenting, 28
    as interval-oriented entities, 89
    sample code and, 17
coding, 26
colon (:), 97, 100
columns, in D, 93, 98
combinations, 101
comma (,), 99, 100
command interpreter, 48
comments, in D, 90, 95
Common Object Request Broker
        Architecture (CORBA), 65
Common Runtime Language, 58
comparators, 114
compiler directives, 12
compilers, 5, 10
    documentation and, 28
completions, 95
component column, 93, 98
component definitions, 93, 96, 98
component groups, 92
component lists, 99
component references, 99
component series, 92
component types, 96
components, 92
components (GUI objects), 63
composed attributes, 32
composition, 3, 31, 32, 35
compound data types, 9
compound statements, 98
concrete classes, 6, 8
condition structures, 90
conditions, 104
configuration file, XML and, 61
connection pooling, 59
constant components, 99
constructor methods, 16
containers, 58
contexts, 61
continuation, 94, 98
control column, 93, 98
controllers, 51
cookies, 56

CORBA (Common Object Request Broker
        Architecture), 65
core logic, in JavaBeans, 66
core logic components, 63
CSS (Cascading Style Sheets), 53, 57
curly brackets ({ }), 106
current-class-defined attributes, 32
current-class-defined methods, 31
cursor, 46

▒D

D, 91–121
    example of, 118–21
    reserved words in, 117
    syntax of, 92–117
data items, 12, 14
    code values in, 90
    XML and, 60
data orientation, xxxii, 87–89
        data-oriented dictionary, 153–78
data relationship management (DRM)
        languages, 89–92
    code examples for. See D, Desc, Descript
data sources, 59
data types, 13–15
    primitive, 9
databases
    algebraic notation for, 84
    design of, 39
    object, 40
    object-oriented, 40
    XML and, 62
decomposition, 37, 41
delimiter keys, 48
dependence, 32, 34
derived classes, 6, 8
Desc
    example of, 147–49
    reserved words in, 144–47
    syntax of, 143–49
Descript, 103
    reserved words in, 140
    syntax of, 129–40
descriptor files, 64
design
    3-tier, 52
    bidirectional, 26, 37
    enterprise-level, 45–68
    function-oriented, 25–44
design patterns, 71, 78
developer class network, 10
DHTML (dynamic HTML), 57
dialogs, 50
directives, 46–52
    document, 66
    undoing multiple, 50

display, 46
DNS (Domain Name System), 54
document directives, 66
Document Object Model (DOM), 56
documentation, 28, 42, 106, 109
    mechanisms and, 33
DOM (Document Object Model), 56
Domain Name System (DNS), 54
domain names, 54
domain reference, 54
double backslashes (\\), 96
double hyphens (--), 93
drag and drop, 50
DRM (data relationship management)
        languages, 89–92
    code examples for. See D, Desc, Descript
drop-down menus, 49
dynamic binding, 33
dynamic composition, 32, 34
dynamic content, 59
dynamic HTML (DHTML), 57
dynamic strings, 102, 113

▓E
e-commerce, 58
echoing, 48
EJB (Enterprise JavaBeans), 64
EL (expression language), 67
encapsulation, 6, 7, 9
Enterprise JavaBeans (EJB), 64
enterprise-level design, 45–68
enterprise software, xxv
entities, 92
    naming conventions for, 94
Entity Beans, 64
entity names, in D, 93
entity references, in D, 94
equation sets, 76
equations, in interaction algebra, 73
evaluation, 48
events (user directives), 51
execution-time state, 40
expression language (EL), 67
expressions, 72
eXtensible HyperText Markup Language
        (XHTML), 61
eXtensible Markup Language (XML), 60–63,
        65
eXtensible Stylesheet Language (XSL), 61
extension interval, 97
external methods, 31
Externalizable interface, 63

▓F
F-keys (function keys), 47
fifth generation process, 65

Filter interface, 66
first generation languages, 11
focus and direct, 50
follow-up steps, 108
forms, 47–50
    added interaction capabilities in, 55–57
fourth generation languages, 11
frames, 53
frameworks, 26
function databasing, 39, 84
function intervals, 97
function keys (F-keys), 47
function orientation, xxvi, 4, 88
    analyzing for, 26
    designing strategies for, 25–44
function-oriented design, core concepts of,
        31
function-oriented languages, 12
    syntax structure, 11, 21
function scoping, 28
function sets, 28
    algebraic notation for, 71–83
    communication among, 38, 42
    network of, 4, 34
functional significance, 37
functions, 28–30
    documenting, 28
    overridden, 6

▓G
glossary, 153-178
GOLD (Goal-Oriented Language of
        Development), 91
granularity, 6, 7
graphical user interfaces (GUIs), 49–52
graphics players, 56
graphics sequencer, 56
group alignment members, 98
group definitions, 98
group member references, 100
group members, 98
groups, 92
GUI interaction, 49–52

▓H
hardware manufacturers, 20
header statements, 92, 96
heaps, 15
help text, 46
high-level languages, 12
HTML (HyperText Markup Language), 53, 57,
        60
HTML tags, 53 ·
HTTP (HyperText Transfer Protocol), 54
HyperText Markup Language (HTML), 53, 57,
        60

HyperText Transfer Protocol (HTTP), 54
hyphen (-), 93

▋I

icons, 49
identification notation, 76
implementation
    functions and, 6
    importance of, 42
    interactive/noninteractive, 48
    programs and, 8
implicit steps, in D, 92–117
implicit variables, in expression language, 67
incomplete strings, 101
incremental sets, 107
incrementation sets, 106
indentation, 94, 98
indirection, 48, 49
inheritance, 3, 6, 8, 31, 32, 35
inherited attributes, 32
inherited methods, 31
initialization, 96, 107, 110, 117
injection, 116
interaction algebra, 33, 71–86
interaction properties, 111
interactive implementation, 48
interfaces, 6, 8, 49
    importance of, 42
    sets of, 38
Intermediate Language, 58
intermediate languages, 6
Internet Protocol (IP) addresses, 54
interval definitions, 96
interval orientation, 88
    in D, 110–15
    in Descript, 136–39
interval/noninterval components, 97
interval references, 103
interval sets, 88
intervals, 88, 92, 97, 109
    as interval-oriented entities, 89
    managed, 93
    naming conventions for, 94
IoC (Inversion of Control), 65
IP (Internet Protocol) addresses, 54

▋J

JAR files (Java Archive files), 62
Java, 12, 57–68
    vs. C++, 18
    vs. D, 118–21
Java 2/Java 2 version 5, 63
Java Archive files (JAR files), 62
Java Database Connectivity (JDBC), 59
.java extension, 57
Java Runtime, 58
Java Virtual Machine (JVM), 58

JavaBeans, 63
JavaScript, 56, 57
JavaServer Faces (JSF), 67
JavaServer Pages (JSP), 65–67
javax.faces package, 67
javax.servlet package, 66
javax.servlet.jsp.tagext package, 66
JDBC (Java Database Connectivity), 59
JSF (JavaServer Faces), 67
JSP (JavaServer Pages), 65–67
JSP custom tags, 66
jumps, 93, 103
JUnit tool, 62
JVM (Java Virtual Machine), 58

▋K

keyboard-only interaction, 45–49
keyphrases/keywords, 93
keystroke pooling, 49
keystroke processing, 48

▋L

labels, 91, 103
languages, 11, 18. *See also* C++; Desc;
        Descript; Java
    C#, 21
    D, 91–121
    DRM, 89–92
    effects on design, 33
    JavaScript, 56, 57
    Objective C, 21
    Smalltalk, 21
    Visual Basic, 22
left angle bracket (<), 97, 102
left square bracket ([), 98, 102
libraries, 6, 8
library templates, 8
line implicit references, 95
lineage, 40
linkage. *See* binding
Listener interface, 66
lists, 99
LiveScript, 56
locaters, 94, 115
logical objects, 6, 8

▋M

Macintosh, 20
Make tool, 62
managed interval definition, 97
managed interval references, 103
managed intervals, 93
management component definition list, 97
management components, 93
mechanisms, 29–33
    documenting, 33
Mediator mechanism type, 34

members (of class), 6, 7
memory address management, in C++, 18
menus, 46
Message Beans, 64
messages
    inherited, 9
    in intermediate languages, 6
    in structured-oriented languages, 7
metalanguages, 53, 60
methods, 31
methods (of handling data), 7
Microsoft, 20
minus sign (-), 101
Model-View-Controller (MVC), 51, 66
models, 51
modes (of interaction), 46
monitor statements, 108
mouse, 49
multicomponent return, 100
multidimensional patterns, 43
multiple inheritance, 32
MVC (Model-View-Controller), 51, 66

N
name equations, 77
name translations, 95
namespaces, in XML, 66
naming conventions, 28, 94
nested condition structures, 90
nesting, interval references and, 104
Netscape, 20
network browsers. *See* browsers
network site servers, 57–65
network sites, 52
network structure, 34
NeXT, 20
nonblock languages, 7
null functions, 30
number sign (#), 100

O
object animation, 88
object databases, 40
object-oriented databases, 40
object-relational (OR) mapping, 40
Object Request Broker (ORB), 65
Objective C, 21
    binding and, 33
objects
    as interval-oriented entities, 89
    logical, 6, 8
    persistent, 6, 8
one-touch directives, 47
OR (object-relational) mapping, 40
ORB (Object Request Broker), 65
overloading methods, 6, 8

P
packages, 6, 8, 92
painting of visual objects, 51
palettes, 50
parallels, 106
parsing, 60
part implicit references, 95
parts, 92
paths, 55
permanent characteristics definition, 96
persistent objects, 6, 8
philosophical balance, 35–43
plug-ins, 56
plus sign (+), 101, 108
point and click, 49
pointers, 64
pointing devices, 49
polling browsers, 54
polymorphism, 6, 8, 9, 31, 35
primitive data types, 9
private usage indicator, 14
procedure orientation, 89
procedure-oriented to data-oriented translation key, 151–52
processing flows, 11, 45–52
product lines, 92
product part completions, 95, 102
product phase sets, 88
product sets, 88, 92, 109
program templates, 6
programming languages. *See* languages
programs, 6
    overridden, 8
prompts, 46, 48
protected usage indicator, 14
proxies (pointers), 64
public usage indicator, 14

R
refactoring, 26
references, 94
reflection, 28, 114
repetitions, 106
reserved words
    in D, 117
    in Desc, 144–47
    in Descript, 140
resource part accesses, 95
resource part references, 106
resources for further reading, 124–126
restarts, 109
return component definitions, 96
return multicomponent definition, 100
right angle bracket (>), 102
right square bracket (]), 98, 102
RTS (run-time system), 5, 51

▓S

scopes, 15, 58, 90
scripting, for browsers, 55
scriptlets, 65
second generation languages, 12
[ ] self execution, 113
semicolon (;), 98
sequence keys, 47
sequences of characters, 47
sequential execution, 38
Serializable interface, 63
serialization, 60
series, 92
series definitions, 98
series member references, 100
series members, 99
server processing, reorganizing, 65–68
servers
    network site, 57–65
    web, 55
servlets, 58, 65
Session Beans, 64
set definitions, 95
set properties, 92
set statements, 92
SGML (Standard Generalized Markup
        Language), 53
sheets (stylesheets), 53
side effects, 97
signatures, 6, 8
site servers, 57–65
Smalltalk, 21
    binding and, 33
software manufacturers, 20
source column, 93, 98
source combinations, 101
spaces, in D, 93
specializable type, 110
square brackets ([ ]), 98, 102
stacks, 15
standard class network, 10
Standard Generalized Markup Language
        (SGML), 53
Standard Tag Library (STL), 66
standardized distributed objects, 64
standardized objects, 63
state, 6, 8, 40
    as interval-oriented entity, 89
statements, 12, 46
    compound, 98
    in D, 92, 93, 96–109
    two-dimensional, 90
static binding, 33
static composition, 32, 34
static content, 59

status count, 108
status monitoring, 108
status name, 108
status table, 108
step definitions, 92, 99
steps, in D, 92–117
STL (Standard Tag Library), 66
string definitions, 99
strings, 101
structure-oriented languages, 7
    syntax structure, 11
Struts, 66
styles (collection of formats), 53
stylesheets, 53
subentities, 72
subscripts, 75
Sun Microsystems, 20
synchronization of objects, 58
syntax, 11
    for D, 92–117
    for Desc, 143–49
    for Descript, 129–40
    interaction algebra and, 71–76, 84
    URI, 54
    variability capabilities of, 68

▓T

tabs, 50
tag file, in JSP 2.0, 67
tag handler, 66
tag library (TL), 66
tag library descriptor, 66
tags, in HTML, 53
tasks (XML-style tags), 62
template feature of C++, 42
Template mechanism type, 30
temporary characteristics definition, 96
testing, automated, 28
text wrapping, 48
third generation languages, 12
threads, 43
    Java and, 58
Tiles, 66
timeline predictions, 44
TL (tag library), 66
toolbars, 50
toolkits, 26
tools
    for application development, 62
    Tiles, 66
trailing vertical slash (|), 93
transfer protocols, 54
transitional code, 106
translation key, 151–52
types, 96

▓U

underscore (_), 104
Uniform Resource Identifiers (URIs), 54
Uniform Resource Locaters (URLs), 54
UNIX, 20
update interval, 95, 112
URIs (Uniform Resource Identifiers), 54
URLs (Uniform Resource Locaters), 54
usage indicators, 14
user-friendly interaction, 46
user request processing flows, 45–52
utilities
    for application development, XML and, 62
    Tiles, 66

▓V

vertical slash (|), 93
views, 51
virtual functions, 30

Visual Basic, 22
visual object interaction, 49–52

▓W

web addresses, 54
web servers, 55
websites, 52
well-formed definitions, 60

▓X

Xerox Corporation, 20
XHTML (eXtensible HyperText Markup
        Language), 61
XML (eXtensible Markup Language), 60–63,
        65
XML Schema, 61
XSL (eXtensible Stylesheet Language), 61
XSLT (XSL Transformation), 61